YEHUDI MENUHIN MUSIC GUIDES

The Trumpet

Crispian Steele-Perkins

D0420554

KAHN & AVERILL, LONDON

First published in 2001 by
Kahn & Averill
9 Harrington Road, London, SW7 3ES.

British Library Cataloguing in Publication Data

A catalogue record for this book is available from the British Library

ISBN 1 871082 69 2

Typeset in Times by YHT Ltd, London
Printed in Great Britain by
Halstan & Co Ltd., Amersham, Bucks

Contents

Acknowledgements

Trumpets are notoriously difficult pictorial subjects, so I am most grateful to my brother, the Reverend Steele-Perkins, who is responsible for the majority of photographs in this book, for the pains he has taken to provide illustrations appropriate to the text.

In the important chapter on 'Posture' I was immeasurably helped by Peter Buckoke, a long-standing colleague as a double-bass player, who has trained and now practises as an Alexander teacher. Also my physiotherapist, Annie Wakeman, has given me exercises to relieve muscular tensions which will now, hopefully, be useful to others.

My publisher has shown endless patience in the process of coaxing this book out of me and has managed to remain sane when confronted by my 17th century approach to spelling (i.e. phonetic!).

It has only been possible to put theory into practice with the utmost forbearance of some of my colleagues. The conductors (alphabetically) Richard Hickox, Christopher Hogwood, Robert King, Andrew Parrot and Peter Seymoor have been especially supportive of my efforts to explore the real sound world of the past, while my good friend and accompanist Leslie Pearson has encouraged me to persevere at times when my cause seemed to be irretrievably lost, for which credit is also due to my long-time, long-suffering assistant trumpeter David Blackadder.

My house-proud wife Jane endures the most excruciating noises and mess whilst I rebuild, and teach myself to play innumerable obsolete and bizarre instruments of the trumpet family. My practise-room is sound-proofed to the outside world but family, guests and pets have for the most part exercised a high degree of tolerance, which is also greatly appreciated.

Introduction

The Trumpet is, by it's nature and design, contrived to attract attention. It therefore symbolises certain extrovert human qualities which do not apply to other musical instruments. In former centuries these attributes comprised heroism, nobility, dignity and triumph; more recently they have also encompassed aggression, vulgarity and bombast.

Before mechanisms were added, the expertise required to play the trumpet was more mystical, since no physical movement was perceptible beyond blowing air into a metallic pipe. The control of the resultant sounds was achieved by minute movements of the facial muscles surrounding the player's mouth. Subsequently, any movement of the hand, fingers or arm gave onlookers the impression that these actions in some way contribute to the creation of the notes; we know, however, that the sound is created by skilfully adjusting the speed at which the lips vibrate, and that valves, slides, triggers and holes only modify those sound-waves which have previously been set in motion in the mouthpiece cup. In the often repeated words of my friend the late, lamented John Wilbraham 'The trumpet makes no sound; the only time it makes a noise is if you drop it'.

In the course of the pages which follow, this theme willconstantly be reiterated, because in the author's opinion, many of the problems encountered by developing trumpeters arise because certain fundamentals are taken for granted, and given little further attention. These principles are:

1. The air-column is caused to vibrate by 'buzzing' into a mouthpiece
2. The pitch of the note is controlled by small, delicate muscles surrounding the mouth and teeth, which are trained and developed to respond with flexibility.
3. These two functions are supported by propelling a column of air from the lungs using a strong muscle called the diaphragm, which separates the lungs from the lower internal organs of the abdomen. Once the control of these activities are co-ordinated, it only remains
4. to push down the right valves at the right time, by which means the intervals between the harmonics are filled.

The quantity of air flowing into the instrument will regulate the loudness of the resultant sounds. It may be observed that it is easier to amplify a passage of music by this means than to reduce it's volume once it is too loud: 'Any fool can play fortissimo , but only an artist dares play pianissimo.'

It is remarkable that the earliest orchestras employed only a handful of stringed instruments, to which were occasionally added a pair of oboes or a pair of trumpets. As the size of the orchestra increased the number of oboes and trumpets usually remained at two whereas other winds were added. The size of the oboe itself remained virtually unchanged, although an increasing number of additional keys supplemented to its original two. To cope with the increased volume required , the size and appearance of the trumpets altered; firstly they became more compact, taking up less space in theatre 'pits' and later adding and experimenting with various mechanical devices which improved intonation, range and security. This fact reveals something rather unexpected about the way in which the trumpet was formerly played. It should be obvious to the intelligent interpreter of repertoire from the Baroque and Classical periods, that a satisfactory balance was customarily sought between the various members of the ensemble; in other words, the trumpet was played surprisingly softly by modern standards. More surprising perhaps, is the balance between obligato trumpet and a solo voice. It is astonishing to find Arias of the utmost delicacy and refinement for Solo Soprano, Solo Trumpet and Continuo among the compositions of Henry Purcell, Alessandro Scarlatti, Antonio Vivaldi, Alessandro Melani and many others.

This strongly suggests to us that when the trumpet was a rigid 7ft (2 metre) tube, the notes were 'coaxed' out of it, and that the problematic 4th and 6th notes of it's scale were 'eased' into consonance by rather gentle blowing into a deep-cupped mouthpiece which essentially lacked stridence. A shallower mouthpiece is necessary to play a shorter trumpet in tune, but with decreasing depth the degree of it's shrillness increases; in this process the high frequency overtones become accentuated, and the fuller 'dark' resonance is lost. Many conductors of Baroque music – themselves an historical anachronism - fail to appreciate this subtle but important detail, and as is observed later, they give us a more Victorian or 'Hollywood-style' perspective on this repertoire as opposed to one enlightened by musical intelligence. I repeat the words 'delicacy' and 'refine-ment' as being the most relevant to this argument.

Equally anachronistically in Victorian England, as we shall see, the 'old' style lingered with the famous English Slide-Trumpet being retained by the traditions of Handelian Oratorio into the first decade of the 20th century. We reach here the pre-cise point at which I separate myself from other writers and per-formers. My own interest in 'historically-aware performance practice' (as it is now rather patronisingly addressed) is in tak-ing surviving specimens 'off the wall' to allow the instruments themselves to show us what they are capable of doing – also what they cannot comfortably do. I regard myself as a musical archaeologist; in pursuit of this interest it has been necessary to expose myself as a hostage to fate, and to act as a human 'guinea-pig' in bringing trumpets back into musical life from the dusty cupboards and cabinets of museums where like idealised infants they are occasionally seen but never heard.

My efforts have by no means always been crowned with

glory – far from it – but with perseverance I believe that occasionally I have been able to offer a glimpse into the past, and have enabled others to share a sound-world that momentarily transcends time. For those who wish to persevere along this voyage of rediscovery I am recalling over the following chapters the information, experimentation and dissemblance of ideas which have accumulated over 35 years. Those who do not share my rather excessive enthusiasm will, I hope, find this book informative nevertheless, and may reflect that there are various ways in which we can enjoy music, no one more or less valid than any other.

To all those aspiring to perform in public on the trumpet, I make three concluding observations. Firstly, there are two types of beings on this planet; those that do things and those that KNOW that they could have done it better! Secondly, I was once greeted after a solo recital in France by an enthusiastic young trumpet student who informed me: 'My teacher told me not to come to listen to you – but I enjoyed it'. (Beware the pedant!).

Finally an anecdote which always makes my eyes moisten (even now as I write it!). In 1956 the great British 'Big Band' conducted by Ted Heath toured the USA. One of the features of their concerts was the duetting of trumpeters Bobby Pratt and Bert Ezzard , of both of whom I was a huge fan. It was after their performance in Pasadena near Los Angeles that Bobby Pratt was making his way out of the stage door of the theatre (he was a well built, but rather shy man) when he was accosted by a diminutive figure, who grasped his hand energetically and effused: 'Mr Pratt, that was just marvellous playing; I truly believe that you must be the greatest trumpet-player in the world'. Somewhat overwhelmed, Pratt replied with customary modesty: 'Oh no, you're very kind, but the greatest player, I believe, is a man called Conrad Gozzo.' The other in his turn was overcome with confusion. 'Why, thank you' said he, 'I am Conrad Gozzo'.

One
Early History

Brass instruments evolved as metallic imitations of primitive lip-vibrated signalling horns. From conch shells, bamboo canes and tree trunks the families of Horn, Trumpet, Trombone and Saxhorn acquired distinguishing features that are comprehensively traced in the well known treatises by Philip Bate and Anthony Baines. From prehistoric times and the earliest Mesopotamian civilisations, through the Empires of the Greeks and Romans, the settlements of Celts and Vikings into the days of the Crusades, it was found that the sound of a vibrating air

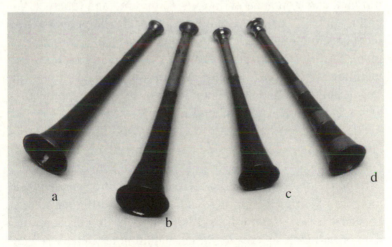

Four English Hunting Horns.
(a)   Köhler and Son, Covent Garden, c.1870
(b)   Köhler and Son, 61 Victoria St., London, c.1896
(c)   Hy. Keat and Sons, 1991
(d)   Swaine and Adeney, proprietors of Köhler and Son, c.1920.
The different length give different pitches, but play only one note each.

1

Replicas of the two trumpets from Tutankhamen's Tomb.
(a) By David Edwards
(b) By the Author.
Twice the length of hunting horns, they produce 2 notes.

column could be effectively amplified by any expanding tube, and that the resultant sound could carry over a great distance. Different shapes and sizes fulfilled a variety of functions from military, ceremonial and religious, to hunting and funereal. We will not identify the many hundreds of species here, but confine ourselves to physical principles and the practical application of them. Suffice it to say that examples of ancient practices and techniques survive in the Australian 'didgeridoo', the Moroccan 'nafir' and the Indian 'karna' which have their equivalents in other societies and civilisations.

The crudest of these is represented by the English Hunting Horn, which varies from 9 inches (23 cm) to 10½ inches (27 cm) capable of producing a single note. The 19th century manufacturer Köhler published a 24 page instruction manual that includes 25 different Hunting 'Calls' (not that different, it must be said!) It is possible for a skilled trumpeter to play a second note or harmonic an octave higher, but all notes in between are totally unobtainable on this short horn. If a similar but slightly longer horn is constructed, the note will sound lower in pitch; if the length is doubled it will sound exactly an octave lower, but the second note an octave higher will be easy to play, furthermore two further notes can be found a fifth higher again, and the third octave higher still; such an instrument is depicted in Egyptian paintings of 3500 years ago, and referred to in hieroglyphics as a 'snb'.

The tomb of King Tutankhamen (died c. 1350 B.C.) yielded two magnificent specimens which are the oldest surviving trumpets presently known. One, of silver, is approximately 23 inches (58.3 cm) long and has a bell like a funnel which is inscribed with the king's name and regimental emblems. It produces the notes exactly as described above as does the copper replica built upon my return from Cairo:

A second trumpet in gilded bronze was severely damaged by a British army bandsman forcing his bugle mouthpiece into it, intending to demonstrate his and its musical prowess. The central section has shattered so that its precise length can only be estimated by measuring along the removable wooden core, which both trumpets have to prevent their thin tubing (0.3 mm) being damaged. Reported measurements of this trumpet give its length between 19½ inches (49.4 cm) and 19¾ inches (50.5 cm); certainly it was considerably shorter than the other, even before the intervention of the British army!

We may assume with some confidence that the trumpets made for Moses (The Book of Numbers, Chapter 10) replicated those which the Israelites had known before their Exodus from Egypt (c. 1000 B.C.) 'And the Lord spake unto Moses, saying "Make thee 2 trumpets of silver: of a whole piece shalt thou make them: that thou mayest use them for the calling of the assembly and for the journeying of the camps".' These, and many other trumpet calls, are proscribed in the Dead Sea Scrolls; again it is likely that they replicate those of ancient Egypt:

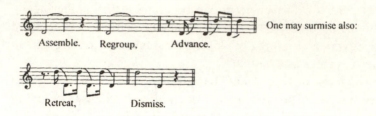

One may surmise also:

Assemble. Regroup. Advance.

Retreat, Dismiss.

It will be noticed that the 'Dismiss' or 'Break Up' has a quality that would not be out of place in a farmyard. The Greek historian Plutarch (47–120 A.D.) confirms this in his 'Morals' (150 and 362) claiming that inhabitants of the Nile Delta hated the sound of the trumpet which reminded them of the braying of the lowliest of animals – an ass (or donkey) when hungry. Composers have subsequently imitated this doleful sound, but none has surpassed these ancient renditions.

Plutarch was of course able to compare this sound to that of the longer Greek 'Salpinx' (approx. 5 feet or 153 cm) whose 'screaming' tone featured in the Olympic games where competitors vied to be heard from a greater distance than their rivals. One, named Achias, having been victorious three times had a column erected in his honour. Plutarch would also have known the straight Roman 'Tuba' which was not dissimilar to the salpinx, also the larger 'G-shaped' 'Cornu' whose 6½ foot (200 cm) to 11 feet (350 cm) of conical tubing wrapped around its player; also the short strident 'Buccina' and wailing funereal 'Lituus' played their parts in the military and civic life of Rome.

Similar instruments have served different cultures all over the world through barbarous and mediaeval times; today many of their direct descendants are still to be seen, their names paying tribute to their humble origins on the heads of cattle. However from the earliest times the trumpet was imbued with ritual and religious symbolism; in biblical times it was sounded only by priests, and in early Christian frescoes it is the prerogative of angels. During the Crusades, eastern influences revived the instrument's fortunes and long straight trumpets appear in pictures of Royal pageants and jousting tournaments. In the 1980's a medieval trumpet was unearthed beneath a lorry park at Billingsgate, London (see Galpin Society Journals XLI, XLIV) whose four dismantled sections are in a remarkably good state of preservation. These sections fit into one another forming a trumpet of some 4¾ feet (144.7 cm).

There is metallurgical evidence that the sections were not all built at the same time, and what looks like a shield-shaped decoration is in fact a patch covering a hole in the bell section. It will not escape notice that within an inch this is the same overall length as a standard military bugle, and of the modern B♭ trumpet and cornet (discounting their valves), therefore whatever notes are playable on the bugle are practicable on the 'Billingsgate' trumpet. Furthermore it is thrice the length of the shorter Tutenkamun trumpet which had only two comfortably obtainable notes, and although there are theoretically other harmonics, reference to the bugle repertoire reveals that in practice the following six (sounding) notes apply:

In part-books and march-cards these notes are generally transposed up a note for simplicity.

The same limit of range applies to the published Coach-Horn 'Calls' of the 19th century; these horns are not dissimilar to medieval trumpets, except that the tubing tapers throughout their length making them horns as opposed to cylindrically tubed trumpets. By the end of the 18th century 342 coaches departed from London to country destinations every day of the week except Sundays (when services were reduced) so the sound of the Coach horn was familiar to urban and rural inhabitants alike. These horns varied from 46 inches (117 cm) to 52 inches (132 cm) in length, we can therefore conclude that over the centuries it was found that the maximum practical yet serviceable length for straight brass instruments was somewhat short of 5 feet (150 cm). It is worth mentioning in passing that

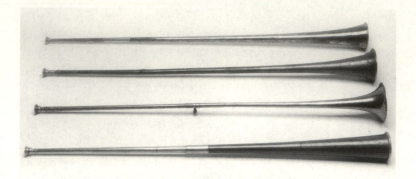

English Coach Horns.
(a)   Anon, c.1910
(b)   Anon. Early 19th Century
(c)   W. Brown, 2 Tracey St., London, c.1908
(d)   Köhler and Sons, 116 Victoria St, London, c.1896
(a) and (b) are solid but (c) dismantles in the middle, and can take an additional
segment, increasing its length by 50%. (d) Telescopes inside itself at the central join.
Beware, There are many fakes in circulation.

shorter horns were available; the long one discussed above served the 'Heavy Mail' drawn by four horses; the 'Beaufort' or 'Tandem' horn served carriages drawn by a pair of horses, this was 36 inches (91.5 cm) long; a short (26 inch, 66 cm) post horn was used in theatres and on bandstands. For easier porterage there were also fully sized coach horns whose sections telescoped inside one another reducing 46 inches to 18 inches (46 cms) and a tightly coiled 'Buglet' folding 52 inches to 6½ (16.5 cms).

The technology of bending or folding metal tubes was developed in the late 13th century and it fostered the innovation of instruments of real musical potential. Lead, which melts at 327° centigrade, is poured into brass, silver or copper tubing (that withstands about 850°C without being affected). When the lead cools, it's consistency is soft enough to be bent, taking the outer harder metal with it. When the desired curve or coil is achieved, buckling can be tapped or kneaded out, the lead again heated enough to melt and to be poured away. This meant that the trumpet could be folded around into a much more portable and convenient shape; it became infinitely more robust and even strong enough to support the weight of a heavy banner – usually emblazoned with the colours and emblems of whichever great nobleman the trumpeter served. The overall length of tubing was increased to over 7 feet (214 cm) which provided a substantially greater range of notes, to such an extent that players specialised in the different registers, the lowest being produced with a large mouthpiece, and the highest often with a shallower one.

Calls for the Hunting Horn published by Kohler & Son (c.1875).

Calls for the Post Horn (may also be sounded on a Coach Horn) published by Chapman and Hall, London, 1888.

7

In ceremonial music, trumpeters played in groups of 4 or 5, with separate parts of which the lowest were rather static 'drones', the middle provided rhythmic impetus, and the highest embellished the harmony with improvisation and ornamentation that became increasingly florid and virtuosic with the passage of time. In the German principalities and the domains of the Imperial Viennese court, powerful Guilds or Brotherhoods were formed for the mutual protection of various trades and skills, amongst them the 'Fellowship of the Trained Bretheren-in-Art' who enjoyed privileged status which they guarded jealously, maintaining severe standards of apprenticeship.

Without conforming and joining this Trumpeters' Guild, it was impossible to gain employment in the Courts or Regiments, or to participate in any way in state functions. The German players exercised a rigorous 'closed shop' purporting to maintain standards, but one wonders, examining records of the names of players employed in various household establishments, whether this was a bare-faced device to keep 'foreigners' out. It is equally interesting to examine English records, which list player's names as far back as the Coronation of Richard III in 1483; there is a sprinkling of obviously non-English names up until the Restoration of the Monarchy in 1660 after which one finds many names sounding Dutch, which is not surprising since King William III was also Prince of Orange. In 1697 alone we encounter Henrick De Vant (later known in the Theatre Royal as Harry Davent) Anthony Ragois, Daniel Le Févre, Bernard van Baton, John Seigneur etc. However, with the Hanovarian kings, less than 20 years later, we find no German trumpeters, even though many attendants, courtiers and military officers flooded across the channel from Hanover – this at a time when the trumpeter's art was at its zenith in the German courts, and Bach was writing some of the greatest music in the instrument's repertory.

There are two explanations of this mysterious situation. Aside from the fact that no musicians in England were retained in full time employment apart from the 24 statutory Royal household musicians (honorary appointments sometimes allocated to non-musicians!) the choir of the Chapel Royal and the 16 State Trumpeters (whose jobs often passed from father to son, and where vacancies occurred irregularly) all other musicians worked freelance relying on private teaching, theatre engagements and the luck to catch the eye of prospective employers

9

or patrons – one wonders what has changed in 300 years!
Nuremburg-made trumpets, used throughout continental
Europe, although following the same principles, differed from
those built by English makers, and the musical results expected
from them were slightly but significantly different. For example Bach's music requires agility and floridity in the third
octave of the trumpet's range, whereas Handel's music, written
for London players, demands greater stamina if less nimble-
ness. German trumpets are constructed with their tubing being

Ceremonial British trumpet with banner (King George V) 1910

held parallel by firm cordage binding the upper sections to a
wooden block, grooved to hold them. The instrument may be
grasped around this binding or held by a small 'knop', the size
of a domestic door-handle, situated half way along the bell section, which helps to reinforce the junction where the cylindrical
tubing fits into the expanding tube of the bell. This knob is
placed also at the point of balance when a banner is suspended
from the instrument. On English-made trumpets it is noticeably
larger (on 17th century trumpets unmistakably so) being not

single but a triple 'ball' through the centre of which the bell section passes. On one side this ball has either holes or grooves which hold the mouthpipe section securely at the point of intersection, giving a self-bracing rigidity that resists damage but which can be dismantled for repair or storage in seconds. This central knop is sometimes called a Pommel' and can be as large as a grapefruit; the distinctive triple knop was retained throughout the 18th, 19th and 20th centuries on British-made fanfare trumpets. These are still heard on state occasions such as the bi-annual ceremony of the Opening of Parliament and at Royal

Six English ceremonial trumpets. From Left to right:
(i)   Reproduction by David Edwards of Simon Beale; copper with silver ornaments (original 1667).
(ii)   Anon. Early Victorian.
(iii)   Potter, London, c.1900
(iv)   George Potter, Aldershott, c.1918
(v)   Henry Keat and Sons, London, c.1942
(vi)   Henry Keat and Sons, Matthias Rd, London, c. 1910

Banquets in England. The double sided banners with the Royal Coat of Arms embroidered in gold braiding weigh about 2 lb and cost £8000 each.

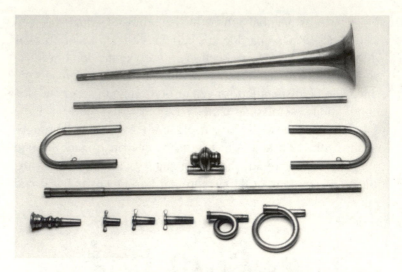

Ceremonial trumpet (George Potter) dismantled
(i) Bell Section (ii) Lower Yard (iii) End Bows (iv) Central Pommel or 'Knop'
(v) Upper Yard or Lead-pipe. (vi) Mouthpiece with 3 tuning shanks and 2 crooks,
one, 1/2 a tone, the other giving a whole tone transposition.

Trumpet (Duty) Calls

One of the very oldest trumpet calls is that heard upon the entry
of the British Monarch on formal state occasions. It is so very
primitive that it may date back to the straight medieval
trumpets. When played in unison by a group of trumpeters,
especially on 'natural' fanfare trumpets, it is extraordinarily
effective. It is written out twice here; firstly as heard nowadays
at the 'Opening of Parliament' ceremony, and secondly as it
appears in John Hyde's (1798) 'Preceptor' for the Trumpet.

Many of these trumpet calls in Hyde's instruction manual are still used in the British army – especially the cavalry.

Bugle (Duty) Calls

Hyde also publishes for the first time the bugle signals used by both the cavalry and infantry who needed to understand clearly the movements each other were making on the field of battle since the one was invariably paving the way for the other. A number of these are included since they make excellent practice material for students. The first flourishes are for the cavalry:

The second are for the infantry:

Two
Early Trumpet Music

We have seen that the trumpet has been used as a signalling instrument for 3500 years at least, and that in its simplest form it is still in use today. It may be said to have found a musical rôle once it was used with other instruments to provide harmony, or to play in consort together ('consort' means partnership or companionship). At its most primitive this was in the form of a drone or sustained note above which a more agile instrument weaves its melodies; the bagpipe achieves this effect on its own, but groups of Indian and Muslim musicians used a lip vibrated drone as far back as the twelfth century, and the European courts adopted their percussion, shawms and trumpets at the same time that a sense of polyphony was being developed in church vocal music. When the trumpet was still straight in the late 13th century, the King of Castille retained four trumpeters, and in England, King Edward III (1327–77) had five. A century later in 1483 for the coronation of King Richard III the Lord Chamberlain's account books reveal 12 'trumpet banners made of sarsynett, with the King's armes £14-16-0' and later that year an order for 'betyng and gylding of forty trumpetts banners' . . . The flourishes they played were not written down but it is probable that they did not always play in unison and that the harmonised fanfare emerged at this time. These, like the military and cavalry fanfares were not written down because the trumpeters were not musically literate and because musical notation was in its infancy; also printing technology (plates first used in 1452: first press set up at Sorbonne in 1470, and in 1476 Caxton's Press started printing in London) was of the future.

15

MUSICAL EXAMPLE 1.

from   "L'ORFEO"   Claudio Monteverdi (1607)

Trumpet 1. Clarino
Trumpet 2. Quinta
Trumpet 3. Alto
Trumpet 4. Vulgano
Trumpet 5. Basso

Played 3 times before the raising of the curtain.

N.B. Clarino with 3 muted trumpets (con sordino).

During the reign of Henry VIII and of his daughter Elizabeth I the Royal establishment maintained between 15 and 18 trumpeters, as other European courts in France, Spain and Portugal did also. Later the German principalities imitated them and it is from Germany and Italy that we have the earliest written and printed

16

guidance to the techniques of playing and to the musical application of them (even though these skills had already been established for several generations). The most articulate revelation of the 'Sound of the Trumpet' corps is encapsulated in the Intrada that precedes the opera Orfeo by Claudio Monteverdi (1607). [See Musical Example I.] It will be noticed that the five trumpets have distinctive rôles to play; the lowest giving a punctuated drone at the beginning of each bar are called Basso and Vulgano, the second sounding the fifth of the chord above the bass' repeated C. The alto has more interesting rhythms, independent of other parts, but plays only the three most comfortable and secure notes, being able to articulate them clearly and safely. The second highest part can use fast clear 'tongueing' but plays slightly higher notes and contributes interesting independent cross-rhythms; the 'clarino' as will be discussed later, adds higher, florid music which became a spectacular art form of its own.

It may also be noticed that there is no part for timpani; in recent years it has become common practice to add drums to all trumpet consort music as was the custom in Germany and at the French court; but it is my strongly-held conviction that this was not necessarily the case in other countries. In London, for example, kettledrums were first introduced at the Restoration in 1660 in imitation of the French court (in 1641 Charles I had sanctioned side-drummers and 'Fifers' into his entourage – as good a reason as any for beheading him I should have thought!). There is evidence that this innovation was received with extreme ill grace by the trumpeters. Purcell used timpani only twice; in June 1692 in 'The Fairy Queen' and months later in the Ode 'Hail, Bright Cecilia' (Nov. 1692) before and after which, for whatever reasons, kettle drums are not included in any of his (clearly written) manuscript scores. I am of the conviction that Purcell knew what he was doing and if instruments such as this are not specified, they should not be added, even if later editions have done so in compliance with subsequent fashion; the notion that large drums and a player

17

were squeezed into the already cramped music rooms and theatre 'pits' to wallop away 'improvising' ad lib for a couple of numbers is too absurd to be considered further; it is astonishing that musicologists have not questioned themselves over this matter for fifty years. Doubtless, it is the perception that the trumpet was a loud (by modern standards) instrument that has misled them. The overwhelming evidence from contemporary sources describing the trumpet being played in a musical context, is one of amazement that it can be played with such refinement and finesse. Godfrey Keller, a young harpsichordist who had been born and raised in Germany, wrote music for Princess (later Queen) Anne's private band, including three sonatas for the famous English trumpeter John Shore. Of the trumpet he wrote that it was '. . . an instrument formerly practised in ye rough consorts of ye field but not instructed in gentler notes, it has learnt to accompany ye softest flutes and can join with the most charming voices'. Shore was clearly an exceptional player (he was also a lutenist); the 'excellent Mr Shoar' as Roger North describes him (c. 1700) for whom Purcell '. . . from his connection with his family, and his admiration of John's performance on the trumpet, took every opportunity in his power to employ him in the accompaniment of his songs and other theatrical compositions'. Sir John Hawkins who wrote these words later in the 18th century also said of him 'by his great ingenuity and application he extended the power of that noble instrument, too little esteemed at this day, beyond the reach of imagination, for he produced from it a tone as sweet as an hautboy (oboe).'

Nothing is told us of the techniques of English trumpeters of this time (there were many of them working in the theatres and playhouses) except that Roger North describes the effect as 'like the chirruping of birdsong'. We only have recourse to surviving Italian and German 'Methods', the earliest two of which make interesting study and the third is a book that no serious student of the trumpet should be without, especially if they wish to perform music of the Baroque era with taste and style.

Cesare Bendinelli (c. 1542–1617) was born in Verona but worked successively in Schwerin, Vienna and Munich; his book *Tutta l'arte detta Trombetta* published in 1614 was probably written c. 1580 and is rare in that it writes out the trumpeter's music and military signals, exercising the five registers encountered in Monteverdi's Intrada. It includes ricercares, intradas and sonatas concluding with ensemble pieces. Altogether these fill 58 double pages. They will not greatly interest the student who only plays modern valved instruments but must have seemed unusually thorough in their day. The second work, *Modo per imparare a sonare di Tromba* was published in Frankfurt for Girolamo Fantini in 1638. It includes three poems in praise of himself; trumpet signals as in Bendinelli's books; balletti, correnti, capprici and sonate for solo trumpet and keyboard (probably harpsichord is intended) and a further 8 sonatas for trumpet and organ. Here we have the trumpet presenting itself as a solo instrument suitable for polite society, and in chamber music. Additionally, there are very detailed exercises in articulation, and instructions on playing those notes outside the limitations of the harmonic series, all of which render this an invaluable document. In 1634 Fantini (who was held in high regard by others apart from himself) gave at least one public concert with the organist Frescobaldi; it is sad to say that unfortunately the latter's abilities as a composer did not rub off on Fantini, whose compositions amount to little more than historical curiosities.

Some of Fantini's technical tricks come as a shock to the modern player. Where trills are marked, it '. . . is performed with the strength of the chest and articulated with the throat . . . ' which denotes a type of 'huffing' on the same note, a technique used to great effect in some of Bach's music. He also says that long notes '. . . should be held in a singing fashion, by starting softly, making a crescendo until the middle of the note, and then making a diminuendo on the second half until the end . . . '
The instructions he gives for articulation seem rather daunting at first:

until one takes it upon trust that Fantini is trying to make one's playing life easier, not more difficult. This is a good exercise for preparing to play with other wind and string instruments, the effects of whose finger movements and bow strokes may require sympathetic adjustments in imitative passages of music, like those accompanying a singer.

The most detailed and important treatise is *An Essay on an Introduction to the Heroic and Musical Trumpeters' and Kettledrummers' Art* by Johann Ernst Altenburg (1734–1801) written c. 1775 but published in Halle in 1795. Writing at a time when the art of 'Clarino' was still flourishing (although its rapid decline occurred before his death) the book expounds the trumpet's history as it was then known and gives a clear picture of apprenticeship, entry into the Trumpeters' Guild, subsequent remunerations to be expected and 'Some suggestions as to how a teacher might appropriately instruct his pupil', all of which make diverting reading. But the passages on 'tonguing', 'trumpet ornaments' and 'The Slide' deserve the attention and study of any potential performer of Baroque music, especially that written for Germany and Austria. All three of the above treatises have been edited for modern publication by the distinguished scholar Dr Edward H. Tarr.

The instrument for which these books were written is known as the Natural trumpet which varied in size from six and a half feet (198 cm) to eight feet (244 cm) in different parts of Europe. They were tuned to the pitch of other instruments by inserting short 'shanks' between the mouthpiece and the apperture where it fits into the trumpet. These shanks usually added 1 inch (2.54 cm) and 1½ inches (3.81 cm) respectively and mounted together they would add 2 inches (5.08 cm) to the overall length of the trumpet, which was sufficient for most contingencies. Sometimes a third shank of 2 inches was supplied which could

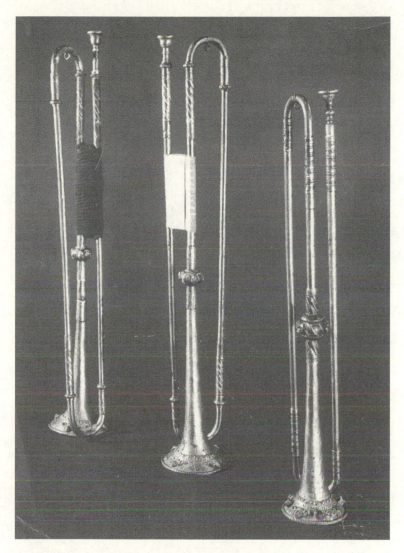

Three 'Natural' trumpets made by members of the Haas family, in Nuremburg. They are longer than English trumpets and bound around a wooden block (concealed).

be built up to a total of 4 inches (10.16 cm) when all three were mounted together. To transpose the instrument, longer shanks coiled into circular or oval shape added ½ a tone, 1 tone or 1½ tones as required, these could also be mounted into one another

An 18th Century English trumpeter (painted by Michael Dahl.) Sometimes thought to portray Valentine Snow, for whom Handel composed many obligati.

giving 2 tones, 2½ tones or 3 whole tones lower. To assign specific pitches to these trumpets is to enter the minefield of disparate pitch across Europe which by the middle of the 18th century varied by as much as a perfect fourth. Some Germanic states such as Cöthen remained at old French theatre pitch (A = 390) whilst at Leipzig the note A sounded half a tone higher (A = 415) in London at A = 439 and in some Italian cities at A = 462. Translating this into our modern (A = 440) standard, the note A would sound as follows in those towns: Cöthen would seem to hear our note G, Leipzig an A♭, London almost an A♮, Italy a B♭. Our A to them would sound as B in Cöthen, as B♭ in Leipzig, fractionally sharp in London and as A♭ in Italy. As if this did not make one's head swim enough, there were different pitches between one church and another in the same city, necessitating the acquisition of sets of instruments to be retained in individual churches. Furthermore the pitch used in churches was usually a whole tone higher than that used in theatres and playhouses. The previously mentioned minor third pitch variation is therefore extended to a fourth. Little wonder that even the most respected of scholars have been confused by Altenburg describing English trumpets as sounding in G, when English players knew them to be built in E or E♭.

The great art of clarino trumpet-playing was not only the art of blending comfortably with other instruments and voices, but in adjusting with the lip those notes of the natural harmonic series that came to be regarded as out of tune. Those notes lie precisely where the laws of physics dictate they should, and they are notes towards which a jazz musician instinctively is drawn. The notes obtainable on a well made natural trumpet are these:

The 'pedal' is virtually never used. The 5th and 7th are a little flat. The 11th harmonic lies between F♮ and F♯ and the 13th is often flat.

The higher partials are unknown in English music, but Bach writes for the 18th and Michael Haydn to the 24th in his Trumpet Concerto in D. From the 17th to the 24th the ascent is in semitones, thereafter in quartertones.

23

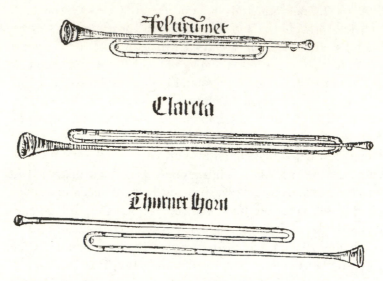

Woodcut depictions from 'Musica Getutscht' by Sebastian Virdung (printed in Basle in 1511) of a standard military 'Field Trumpet', the 'Clareta' or 'Clarino' for playing in 'singing style' in the upper register and the 'Thurner Horn' whose upper tubing 'telescopes' to form a single slide which extends sufficiently to play non-harmonic notes in melodies such as chorales or hymn tunes. These instruments were used in different contexts by municipals musicians who were often required to ring the quarterly and hourly bells, and to raise the alarm in the event of fire or the approach of hostile armies. They performed music from the church and city towers, at celebrative functions such as weddings and feast days; also at funerals and banquets. To avoid excessive exploitation they formed themselves into Guilds or 'Brotherhoods'.

Although players claim to reproduce the sounds and techniques of the past, the truth is that at the time of writing, no trumpeter living has achieved recognition as being able to perform with consistent accuracy music such as the first trumpet part of Bach's *Magnificat* or *Mass in B Minor* without recourse to modifications such as finger holes. This is not to deny that impressive demonstrations may be heard in the tolerant environment of academic institutions, but to admit that audiences, conductors and record producers (let alone other instrumentalists) are not sufficiently impressed with what they hear to consider the exercise worth pursuing. The discerning record or CD collector will have isolated examples where the real sound of a Natural trumpet may be sampled, but when Don Smithers began a series of records for Philips in the 1970's, his stupendous achievements were abanonded as being inconsistent and too time-consuming in production to be economically viable. Since then, Baroque trumpet music has been heard upon vented trumpets which deliver security and intonation that satisfies 20th century standards and tastes, but which eliminate the overtones which give a distinctive timbre to any brass instrument of long tubing – this quality or 'frissance' has been the target of brass instrument manufacturers for the last 50 years, so that horns, trumpets, trombones and tubas are made of much wider tubing and (except for trombones) are shorter, higher pitched instruments than those played earlier in the century. However, the trumpeters of the Royal Household Cavalry may still be heard sounding Natural Fanfare trumpets. Moreover only one generation separates myself through Ernest Hall, to his teacher Walter Morrow who still retained his old 'Slide' trumpet for Handelian performances such as *Messiah*. These instruments were a perfected Natural trumpet used in British orchestras throughout the 19th century. It was the first trumpet to be mechanised.

Three
The Slide-Trumpet

From the early 15th century there is evidence that instruments of the trumpet family were used in a musical context with other instruments, and that restrictions of range were overcome by the use of a slide. The effective length of such a trumpet's tubing could be instantly increased by the telescopic action of inner and outer sections of mouthpipe being extended and withdrawn over one another. Later in the century these cumbersome movements were halved by the development of double slides that ran parallel to one another; new, nimbler techniques earned this 'pumping' mechanism the soubriquet 'sackbutt' and from it developed the familiar trombone.

The single slided trumpet is illustrated in many contemporary paintings and frescoes usually accompanying a pair of shawms (a double-reeded precurser of the oboe). This group was known as an Alta Ensemble and the players were referred to as the Haut (Loud) Menestrels. They provided music during processions and banquets also for dancing; surviving manuscripts indicate that the trumpet played a sedate 'Cantus Firmus' over which the shawms play more elaborate and decorative music, an example of this is the Alta Danza by Francisco de la Tor.

Experimental reconstructions suggest that the slide was capable of being extended sufficiently to lower the pitch of each harmonic through five positions to two whole tones. This does not give a fully chromatic compass but enables the instrument to obtain many additional notes. Various sources refer to the medieval slide-trumpet as 'minstrels trumpet' as opposed to that used for ceremonial or military service.

Alta Danza: Francisco de la Tor.   (Transcribed by C. Steele-Perkins)

(Cancionero musical de Palacio, Madrid).

Sebastian Virdung's famous woodcut of 1511 illustrates the functions as much as the shape and size of trumpets of the time. The basic 'Felttrumet' of the army, the melodic 'Clareta' and the slide 'Thurner Horn' of the municipal musicians served different functions and were accorded widely differing symbolic rôles and status. The Waites and City trumpeters were expected to play many instruments in the course of their duties (specialisation being a concept of the future) and amongst the string, wind and keyboard accomplishments for which they were tested before being appointed, they were required to play the minstrel's or Zug (German for slide) trumpet. Early references to the use of these are as follows:

In 1415 at the Council of Constance, the Earl of Warwick engaged three trumpeters who processed on the feast day of St. Thomas of Canterbury playing 'in three parts as one customarily sings'.

28

In 1418 Charles VI of France employed Hermen as 'Trompette pour Menestrier'.

In the 1420's Canon Gerson of Notre Dame wrote of the trumpet being used in church with the organ, also occasionally other wind instruments were played during services.

From 1422–1462 the Burgundian Court made payments to several 'Trompettes de la Guerre' and to a single 'Trompette des menestrels'.

In 1423 the Court of Aragon in Spain employed a 'Trompeta Bastarda' as trumpeter of the minstrels.

In 1425 the Burgundian court purchased a set of shawms for 14 livres and for 10 livres a trumpet 'for serving with the minstrels'.

c. 1455 the Bible of the Duke Borso of Ferrara depicted a sliding trumpet with shawm and bombard in an Alto Ensemble.

In the 16th and 17th centuries the Tower musicians and Stadtpfeiferein (German for City 'Pipers') of the Holy Roman Empire played the single slide trumpet literally from dawn to dusk. Their duties included the playing of an early morning chorale (as early as four o'clock in the morning in the city of Lübeck, according to Dr. Edward H. Tarr) whilst labourers went to work; again at noon during their lunch break and at nine in the evening when the day ended. In between they would play at dinners for the City council and other festivities throughout the day. In England it may be assumed that musicians fulfilled similar duties, including the custom of providing two trumpeters to play a fanfare to announce the arrival of the circuit judge at the County Assize courts (these would be ordinary fanfare trumpets) and their responsibilities also included the important function of watchman, when in the event of an outbreak of fire, the populace were to be alerted to the danger. Duties such as these can be traced back to the 12th century, and surviving instruments like the Moot Horn in the City of Winchester (c. 1180) can be examined and even blown.

In Leipzig at the end of the 17th century, an outstanding trumpeter called Johann Pezel achieved a formidable reputation

A Flatt-Trumpet with two shawms. Florence c.1480

both as player and composer. His numerous sonatas, intradas and dance movements for consorts of trumpets, trombones and cornetti give us a clear idea of the music that was performed by the municipal players, and the high standard of artistry that was heard daily. Pezel was succeeded as senior trumpeter and 'stadtmusicus' by Johann Christian Gentzmer upon whose death in 1719 the memorable clarinist Gottfried Reiche was promoted to the post. For him Bach was to compose most of his formidable output for the high trumpet, and also chorales and obligati that could only have been played upon a slide-trumpet. Recent research has revealed that when he died in 1734, Reiche left several trumpets, including two with slides (but not a coiled trumpet as featured in Haussmann's famous portrait of him). Upon these he would have played not only the trumpet part of his own compositions:

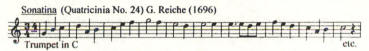

Sonatina (Quatricinia No. 24) G. Reiche (1696)

Trumpet in C   etc.

but also the chorales from Bach's cantatas that played notes that could not feasibly have been 'lipped', such as the well known melody *Jesu, Joy of Man's Desiring* or the following:

J.S. Bach (BWV 167) No. 5 Choral

Clarino in C   etc.

(BWV 24) No. 3

etc. (Bar 90)

31

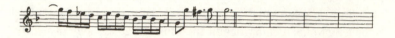

For Bach to have persisted in writing such demanding music he must have greatly appreciated Reiche's astonishing technical dexterity not only in his high clarino register but upon his surprisingly agile slide-trumpet also.

By this time the double slided trombone (or sackbut) was well established as a musical entity in its own right, but it had been regarded as a type of trumpet by commentators and diarists just as a young child would nowadays point at a tuba and exclaim 'Look at that big trumpet'. There has been some confusion therefore when referring to the more obscure brass instruments that were only used occasionally. One of these appears in Bach's scores as the corno da tirarsi or slide-horn, and scholars appear baffled as to how this instrument functioned. Certainly it may well have been played by a musician who doubled on the trumpet (even Reiche himself) but one with nimble technique:

J.S. Bach (BWV 162) No. 1

Tromba in C (Corno da tirarsi)

The other instrument that has been misunderstood, mainly because of its misleading name, is the English 'Flatt' trumpet which Henry Purcell used in his Funeral Music for Queen Mary II. However it is vividly described by James Talbot, a contemporary writer of Purcell's time, who painstakingly measured many musical instruments of the period, and whose verbal account accords with pictures of the time of a trombone-like instrument whose rear bow can be drawn out behind the player's left ear, to play chromatically if not particularly fast.

Musical Example 3

DEAD MARCH - Sounded before the Queen's Chariot. (Played in front of the Funeral Bier in Westminster Abbey).

CANZONA (H. Purcell) for 4 Flatt-Trumpets. (Sounded after the Anthem).

Like the trombone, or possibly before it, the instrument may well have symbolised the soul's descent into purgatory, and Purcell used it in this context when he added 'Flat' trumpets to the fifth act of Thomas Shadwell's play *The Libertine* when it was revived in 1695. The chord sequences are the same in both funeral marches, but the canzona heard at Queen Mary's internment is unique, and in peformance sometimes marred by the intrusive insertion of kettledrums which make neither harmonic nor musical sense: as previously stated, Purcell did

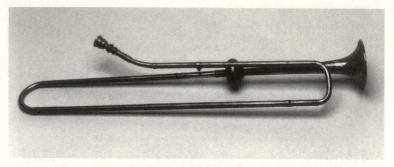

Reproduction of a 'Flatt' trumpet; made by the author in 1990.

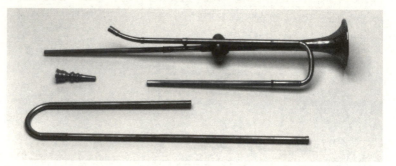

'Flatt' trumpet dismantled; with mouthpiece and slide removed.

not provide a drum part and therefore clearly did not want one. In fact timpani are generally associated with the martial fanfare trumpets, not with trombones or their relatives, and one should no more think of adding them here than in beefing up the statue's coming to life in Mozart's *Don Giovanni* (the first entry of the trombones).

The memory of these mournful funeral trumpets evidently lingered amongst the English trumpet-playing fraternity, for although the untempered Natural trumpet was played exclusively throughout Handel's career in London, by the end of the 18th century the universal adoption of equal temperament and the increased volume of larger orchestras, rendered the bending or lipping of problematic harmonics impracticable and unacceptable. Therefore in response to criticisms the principle of lengthening the tubing (thereby altering the pitch) by extending the rear bow of the trumpet backwards towards the player, was reintroduced. The credit for this ingenious device has rightfully been given to the trumpeter John Hyde, whose 'Preceptor' of instruction has been previously quoted, and hundreds of surviving specimens bear testimony to the success and effectiveness of an instrument that was used for nearly a century, but in almost no other country except the British Isles. The reason for this phenomenon is that the Handelian legacy became a way of musical life in England – it is still said that in the north of the country there are only three seasons instead of four; Spring, Summer and Messiah. The various musical festivals in Norwich, York, Leeds, Worcester, Gloucester and Hereford always had an oratorio by Handel for the choirs to join in and isolated songs such as 'Let the Bright Seraphim' from *Samson*, 'Revenge Timotheus Cries' from *Alexander's Feast* and 'The Trumpet Shall Sound' from *Messiah* were featured on programmes in the Pleasure Gardens, spa salons and public concerts throughout the country (and still are!). As other ingenious mechanical developments were introduced, such as keys and valves, they were invariably judged to detract from the robust nobility of the trumpet's tone, and the eventual alternative – the piston cornet – was regarded as a derisible, unacceptable option.

The prototype conversion of a brass Natural trumpet made by Rodenbostel, with a retractable rear bow (for improved intonation) made by Richard Woodham still survives in private ownership. Other early specimens have the same, surprisingly refined mechanisms including a pair of clock springs and a notched tuning device whose functions have only recently come to be understood. Hyde's original trumpet was restored by Peter Barton who has also assisted the author in the refurbishment and rebuilding of more than twenty early trumpets in the process of which we have both learned a great deal. The Woodham-Rodenbostel instrument was devised in about 1790 and English trumpets were available with clock-springs for more than sixty years.

7 English slide-trumpets. All are crooked in D at A=415.
(a)   A late 18th Century ceremonial trumpet converted to the earliet clock-spring
mechanism with tuning 'notch'. The bell, by Henry Keat and Sons, is a replacement.
(b)   A clock-spring model with tuning 'notch', but with longer extensions of the rear
bow. The bell by Hawkes and Son is a replacement.
(c)   Charles Pace, London (c.1840) compression-spring model. The central rod,
manipulated by the right hand, is unsupported.
(d)   Anon (probably Goodison) compression-spring trumpet.
(e)   Köhler and Sons, 35 Henrietta St., Covent Garden, London (c.1860) 'T.Harper-
improved', elasticated (rubber)-spring model.
(f)   W.D. Cubitt & Sons & Co, London (1885) metal-spring slide trumpet.
(g)   F. Besson, 198 Euston Rd, London (c.1880). Metal-spring trumpet, with tuneable
front end bow.

As the 19th century progressed other, simpler springs became available, but the principle of withdrawing and returning a U-shaped rear bow by means of a telescopic pulley remained the same. Half a tone was judged sufficient to give the trumpet additional notes, and to correct the 11th and 13th harmonics; only in the second half of the century were efforts made to lower the pitch by a whole tone or more. Three stages of evolution have been identified with the 'Return' spring. Firstly a clock spring in a metal box or barrel round which a gut cord reached along the telescopic central tube to be attached to the cross bar that held the retractable U-bend. When extended the cord was threaded and knotted into a small hole in the barrel, and as the rod slid back to its closed position the barrel rotated and wound the cord around its exterior. In the event of this jamming, a second spring-box could be activated by fitting a spare gut chord into a groove on the finger-pull which would fulfill the same function until the player had time to dismantle and repair the fault. This cannot be done without unscrewing the spring box and dismantling the entire mechanism, but from personal experience, this is mercifully an uncommon occurrence. The exterior cord does not pull the rod back as evenly and was therefore only used in such emergencies.

In the 1840's a compression-spring model was designed and introduced by the London maker Charles Pace. Here the spring is moved back between the legs of the sliding rear-bow, and as the central rod is drawn back the spiral spring around it is compressed or squeezed, and upon release it returns the rod and slide to closed position.

In the second half of the 19th century, the ability to make a tight narrow metal spring enabled manufacturers to insert this inside the central tube to provide the simplest and most efficient return mechanism. On some models a rubber chord was used instead, but even in the 1860's some players persisted in ordering from Köhler and Hawkes trumpets furnished with the old-fashioned double clock springs.

There were also devised various ways of tuning these trumpets to the pitch of the orchestra. During the 18th century small tuning shanks were universally employed to extend the length of the trumpet's mouthpiece, thereby lowering the pitch of the

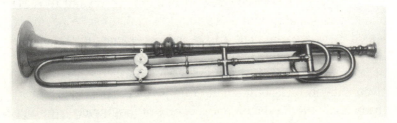

Late 18th Century slide-trumpet, made in London.

The Author in action.

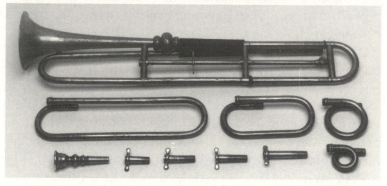

Köhler slide-trumpet (c.1860) with all accessories. Trumpet, 4 crooks, 4 tuning shanks and mouthpiece.

instrument. Slide trumpets were built in the key of F and provided with crooks that lowered its pitch to the keys of E, E♭, D and C and usually with three tuning shanks that respectively added one inch, one and a half and two inches to the instrument's overall length; these could also be mounted into one another (as could the crooks) to give further permutations. Eventually the very best quality trumpets were provided with as many as six tuning shanks and a choice of mouthpieces for high or low register.

The very earliest models of slide trumpet were equipped with a further tuning device of extraordinary subtlety. The instrument is braced and held rigid by a central cross bar through which the telescopic central tube passes. Behind this, where the compression-spring was later fitted, a rotating collar with five grooves cut into it, fits around a portion of the central tube from which protrude five small 'teeth'. The grooves normally slot around these teeth leaving the slide in closed position, but they can be adjusted to fit around either four, three, two, one or even around

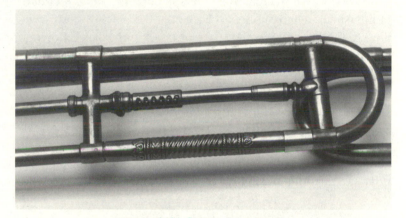

Detail of 18th Century tuning 'notch'

Köhler trumpet and accessories in their box or 'chest'.

no teeth at all, each time holding the slide ⅕th of an inch further out since the teeth are spaced ⅕th of an inch apart (½ a cm). Working with later slide trumpets it seemed very convenient that once tuned to the orchestra in one key, the mouthpiece and tuning shanks were transferred to other crookings thereby staying tuned to the orchestra. It thus seemed inconvenient on the early models that with decreasing sizes of crooks incremental lengthening of the tuning shanks was needed. Eventually I realised that for each crooking the notches also had to be adjusted accordingly to give a perfect half tone when the slide was fully retracted. When this is done the same length of tuning shank again applies to each key, the notches corresponding to the descending sequence of crookings from F down to the key of C.

The abandonment of this device may have been one of the 'improvements' incorporated into the trumpets marketed by Clementi and Köhler in collaboration with the great mid-19th century trumpeter Thomas Harper – it may have seemed preferable to retain a longer extension of the slide. Certainly in Harper's Tutor (published in 1837) he states that with the slide fully extended the notes low B♭, low D, and G♯, F♮ in the stave

are obtainable as passing notes (insinuating that they are partially 'lipped' and not effectively sustained). In his son's 'School for the Trumpet', notes requiring a whole tone shift in the slide are expected to be practised in crookings from F to D but not below. He writes the notes G♯, F♮ in the stave and D♮ below it, as a matter of course:

Thomas Harper (Jun.) School for the Trumpet. Exercise 63.

Allegro moderato

40

The above exercise shows that surprising agility was acquired by Harper and his pupils. This may have also been sought by the forward moving slides patented by the Frenchman Legram in 1821 as played by Dauverné in the 1830's, also as on the trumpet played by the German Buhl and those made by Hattenhof of Hanau and Saurle of Munich; but they failed in competition with valves. The outstanding feature of the English slide-trumpet as Art Brownlow points out in his definitive book *The Last Trumpet* (Pendragon Press, Stuyvesant, New York) was that it retained the dignity of tone of the Natural trumpet so essential to the interpretation of the repertoire of Purcell and Handel. It also suits all the music of the 'classical' period and all Baroque music except the most florid, where it is handi-capped by the larger, deeper mouthpieces traditionally used in England. The change in perception of what was deemed to be desirable in regard to trumpet tone, may be traced to a performance in London in 1888 of Bach's *Mass in B Minor*.

It should be born in mind that Victorian England had a confi-dence and arrogance that swept conventions aside that were in the path of 'progress' (municipal planners had torn down the old medieval walls of all but three of the country's provincial cities – also most Jacobean country houses had been refaced, or defaced, with facades and extensions to Victorian taste). The above-mentioned concert was reviewed by Bernard Shaw who highly praised the trumpet playing of Walter Morrow upon his long, straight 'Bach' trumpet constructed for him with two valves by Messrs. Silvani and Smith (the claim that it was an 'authentic' instrument was clearly bogus, since valves were only introduced in the 1840's). Shaw expressed disappointment that his colleagues Backwell and Ellis '. . .blew sedately into their desks upon their old slide-trumpets.' The old unforced 'clarino' sound was thus invalidated and dismissed for nearly a centry until it was decided to reassess the internal balance of the orchestra.

Four
The Keyed-Trumpet and Keyed-Bugle

The principle of altering the pitch of notes upon the trumpet by uncovering a hole placed at a strategic point along its tubing was not applied until the end of the 18th century, although for centuries trumpeters had played alongside shawms, oboes, cornetti and flutes which relied upon them. The earliest surviving example that survives may be seen in the Museum of London and is fully described in Eric Halfpenny's 1960 article for the Galpin Society Journal (No. XIII). Made for the private orchestra of King George III by William Shaw in 1787 of hallmarked silver, it is in its original box with all crooks and tuning shanks; sadly in recent years its original mouthpiece has been stolen. It stands in the pitch of E♭ (at A = 439, virtually modern pitch as explained previously) and has crooks to D, C and B♭, also the four tuning shanks add ½ inch (1.27 cm) 1 inch (2.54 cm) 1½ inches (3.81 cm) and 2 inches (5.08 cm) respectively to its length. The unique feature of this instrument is that its lower yard is perforated with four holes of approximately 0.15 inches (0.38 cm) width, three of which are covered by rotating collars, and the fourth, being out of the player's reach has a long key covering it like that of a clarinet. Each hole relates to one crook at a time and when uncovered raises the pitch of the harmonic series by a fifth. The hole nearest the player affects the instrument whilst in E♭, in other words before crooks are added. The next hole along relates to the smallest (D) crook, the next to that in C and the hole covered by a key is used for the crooking B♭. When playing in C for example, whilst the hole is closed by placing a finger over the otherwise exposed hole, the normal

42

'natural' harmonics are obtained:

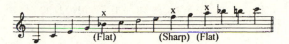

but when the finger is raised exposing the hole, the air column inside the trumpet ceases to vibrate at that point (which is a 'nodal' point) and the sound of each harmonic is raised by a fifth:

One would expect the note F to be flat since it is the normally low' seventh harmonic but in fact in each key it produces an excellent note; the new 11th harmonic of high C is unusually sharp however and that note must be played 'naturally' with the hole closed.

The new range of this 'Harmonic' trumpet is therefore considerably enhanced and the intonation greatly improved; therefore it is accurate and secure in performance. Between these two series of notes the player could produce the following notes – those requiring the hole to be opened are marked with an 'O':

In E♭ and D the same results pertain and are highly satisfactory but in B♭ (in the author's opinion) the hole is a little too small and the instrument resonates less well when the key is raised.

It is notable that by the time that Haydn visited London for the first time (1791–2) both this trumpet and the slide-trumpet of John Hyde were in use, and he most probably heard both of them. The need to improve the trumpet's intonation had been prompted by Charles Burney's criticism of the 1784 Handel

Centenary Commemoration Concerts, in which he praised the playing of James Sarjant but noted that whenever he sustained the fourth or sixth notes of his scale (the 11th and 13th harmonics) the audience visibly winced. The 'Harmonic' trumpet cures these ills but a reproduction of it revealed that once tuning shanks are added to it, the holes are not exactly on the precise 'nodal' point of the tubing and therefore the notes employing the vent-holes become stuffy and do not respond properly. For this reason one can assume that the system was

(i) E♭ trumpet with 3 keys (made by Robert Vanryne)
(ii) E♭ hand-stopped trumpet, crooked into C.

Trumpet in E/E♭ with 5 keys (R.Vanryne)

not generally adopted. Had they thought to adjust the fine tuning by sliding the whole lower yard and rear bow as modern Vented Baroque-style trumpets do, it might have been another story. As it was, the slide-trumpet prevailed since the quality of all its notes retained the vigour and purity of the 'natural' sound.

It is not improbable that when Haydn returned to Vienna, he discussed the 'harmonic' or 'vented' trumpet with the eminent trumpeter Anton Weidinger. As far back as the 1760's horn players had experimented with keyed instruments, and a Dresden trumpeter in the 1780's had experimented with the idea, but discarded it due to the uneven tone produced. By 1793 Hessman, a young amateur trumpeter in Hamburg claimed to have invented a chromatic instrument but it was undoubtedly thanks to the perseverance of Weidinger that a trumpet with three (and later with four or five) key-covered holes was perfected. It was for Weidinger's newly invented trumpets that two of the best-loved concertos for the trumpet were composed, one by Haydn in 1796 and the other by Hummel in 1803.

The prototype keyed-trumpet has not apparently survived. Contemporary commentators suggest that Weidinger was very secretive about it, but copies of later instruments give us a very clear idea of what the technical and musical capabilities of his instrument were. By 1790 trumpets built in the twice folded format of a modern 'Duty' E♭ trumpet were not uncommon. The tubing needed to be perforated with only three holes to be almost fully chromatic throughout its range. A fourth hole is only essential for a low B♮ which is significantly absent from Haydn's Concerto. Depending upon the degree of expansion in the instrument's bell section, the holes (which are to be covered by keys) were made approximately 9 inches (23 cm) back from the bell, which would raise all the harmonics by half a tone, a further 4 inches (10 cm) gives a second semitone higher and a further 5 inches (13 cm) finds a hole that will raise the fundamental harmonics by a minor third (or three half tones). These three holes will in theory now produce the following scale of notes: x indicates notes played with all holes closed, 1 represents those played with the hole nearest the bell opened, 2 with the next in line that raises the notes by a whole tone and 3 with the hole producing a minor third:

A fourth hole placed 6½ inches (16.5 cm) further back – usually on the back bow of the bell section – gives the low B♮ and (although it shouldn't) an excellent F♮ at the top of the stave. Later models give alternative keys for the very first hole which offers some necessary options for intonation.

Hummel's Concerto requires, in the 141st bar of the first movement, a low F♯ below the stave which can be 'lipped' down from a low G, but if it is to be sounded properly it requires a key placed considerably further back along the tubing; in theory 27 inches (69 cm) from the bell but in practice more like 30 inches (76 cm) where the note can be played as a fundamental – albeit somewhat fuzzily. It is the author's belief that Weidinger's second instrument was constructed in E♭ like the first but had a key at the bell end that remained open unless closed by the use of a key (as happens on a keyed-bugle). The tuning of the resultant trumpet would therefore appear to rise half a tone to E, and the end key could be closed to give a good low F♯ (sounding A♯ or B♭) and the notes of the arpeggio of B♮

on the instrument which would have given better tuning and improved resonance to many important notes. The tone of such a trumpet would also be more even than the one designed upon the previously described system.

The keyed-trumpet was successful for a while as a solo instrument but it was never accepted into the symphony orchestra because it lacked the penetrating ring of a true trumpet, and it's tone at best is more like that of a woodwind instrument. It was used in Italy, particularly in town bands, and in the theatres and opera houses in which the municipal musicians also performed. The instruments that survive are generally built in the key of G or A♭ and have a key placed between what has previously been described as the 3rd hole (producing a written E♭) and the 4th (giving low B♮ and high F♮). This additional key gives the missing harmonics upon the written chord of E♮. These trumpets were evidently crooked into the various keys that one encounters in the music of Italian opera composers, and each crooking demanded different fingering to produce acceptable intonation. This was achieved by the best performers such as the Gambati brothers who played for some time in the King's Theatre, London in the 1820's. Their tone was described as coarse and raw even though the playing was very accurate; in London, most of their colleagues preferred the traditional sound of the slide-trumpet, and by the time that Allesandro Gambati began playing in the new Italian Opera House in New York in November 1833, he had begun playing a trumpet with two piston valves.

More widespread use was made of another keyed soprano instrument that was developed from the infantry bugle by the Irish bandmaster, Joseph Halliday. In 1810 he was granted the patent for an instrument initially with five keys which he called (in honour of the Commander-in-Chief of the armed forces – the Duke of Kent) the 'Royal Kent Bugle'. The original design was pitched in C, and the five keys raised the basic bugle harmonics:

in steps by half a tone, a whole tone, a minor third, a major third and a fourth respectively; the sharpened fourth was played by opening the fourth and fifth holes together. Within a very short time, the bell had been lengthened to take a closing-key that lowered the pitch from C to B and a crook was provided that lowered the bugle to B♭. The fingering remains almost the same in both keys although the thumb-operated note that should produce the minor third of the scale requires the adjacent (one tone) key to be opened at the same time to raise it from a rather sharp 'D'. On some later models a key between this and the major third key was fitted to give E♭ and B♭ in the stave, to be played by either hand. Eventually up to ten keys were available, but the majority of the early examples have six and this sufficed for the requirements of most band musicians.

The second and third fingers of the right hand rest on a bridge covering the passageway of the index finger's key. This key produces a better top C on most models than that obtained with no keys pressed down.

Fingering system for the Royal Kent Bugle with six keys

⊗ Denotes the terminal key being closed by the little finger of the right hand
O Denotes no keys pressed at all
1 Indicates the ½ tone hole opened by the right hand's 3rd finger
2 Indicates the tone hole operated by the right digit (1st) finger
3 Requires the thumb of the right hand to open the 1½ tone hole: it is recommended that the index finger key is also opened
4 Is the key for a major 3rd and is opened by the left hand's thumb
5 Is ½ a tone higher and requires the left hand index finger

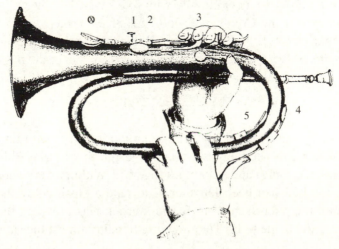

The Duke of Kent responded favourably to the instrument being named in his honour, and the British regimental bands adopted it with alacrity (the Duke was King George III's fourth son). One of the first musicians to master the new instrument was the clarinetist Thomas Willman who played in his own benefit concert in Dublin on May 30th 1811 'a Concerto upon the improved patent Kent bugle horn'. The performance was repeated on June 14th in Dublin's Theatre Royal. Willman subsequently moved to London where he played principal clarinet at the King's Theatre; he was also Bandmaster of the Coldstream Guards from about 1816 to 1825 which was a highly influential post. (His brother who remained in Ireland was described in Michael Kelly's 1826 memoirs as 'The finest trumpet player I ever heard in any country . . . his execution on the instrument almost baffled belief.')

In 1815 after the Battle of Waterloo, the victorious armies marched into Paris where the British regimental bands impressed audiences to such an extent that French, German and Italian manufacturers replicated the keyed-bugles which thereafter became established throughout Europe and North America as an important soprano ingredient of musical groups. The emerging amateur wind bands in England, such as Besses-o'th'-Barn, enrolled their services; by 1818 John Clegg played the keyed-bugle alongside the clarinets, piccolo, trumpet (most likely slide-trumpet) two horns, trombone, two bass horns and bass drum. These instruments were not supplanted by valved instruments until 1849.

The opera houses also welcomed the new sound. As early as 1813 Henry Bishop's opera, *The Miller and His Men*, stipulated that the first trumpet 'change to keyed-bugle' for the 'Arietta' and 'Bohemian Waltz' sections of the overture where the instrument takes the solo melodic line. Like the trumpet part at this point, the pitch required is C, and personnel lists tell us that the player was Thomas Wallis who is recorded in the membership documents of the Royal Society of Musicians (7 Aug 1808):

'He is engaged as first trumpet as the Theatre Royal Covent

Garden and the Little Theatre Haymarket and as first horn ('trumpet' inserted over 'horn') at the oratorios, Covent Garden.' Theatre Royal accounts reveal that later he was paid nine shillings and twopence as a salary during the opera season and that this was supplemented by five shillings each evening when he was required to 'double' on the keyed-bugle. The instrument remained requisite for theatre trumpeters in England and Ireland for the next forty years. It was popular throughout Europe also, although in France and Germany the design and layout of the instrument was slightly different. One may judge the technical fluency expected from the following excerpt from a 1829 arrangement of Beethoven's Septet in F:

In England the keyed-bugle became a commonplace musical instrument. As early as 1814 the Black Dyke Mills Band used two; the regimental bands placed them conspicuously on the right-hand side although the soprano line was carried mostly by flutes, clarinets and oboes. In the early 1820's the Royal Artillery Band carried 2 flutes, 3 oboes, 11 clarinets, 3 bassoons, 2 French horns, 2 trumpets, 3 keyed-bugles, 3 trombones (alto, tenor and bass), ophicleide, 2 bass horns, 2 serpents and 5 drummers. The firm of Clementi advertised amongst other musical wares in 1823:

Patent Kent Bugle, 6 keys £6-6-0
Patent Kent Bugle, 7 keys £7-7-0
Patent Kent Bugle, 8 keys £9-9-0

Brass mouthpieces cost 4 shillings. If silver-plated they cost an additional shilling and for the same price (5 shillings) one could be supplied in ivory.

The famous Cyfartha Band from the ironworks at Merthyr Tydfil (formed in 1838) was still using 3 keyed buglers in about 1855 but by that time the valved cornet had supplanted most of its competitors for the soprano parts of band music. The keyed bugle was not uncommon in use for entertaining passengers of long distance stage coaches. Dickens makes references to this custom in his novels, notably the *Pickwick Papers* and *Martin Chuzzlewit*. Although editions of treatises on orchestration still referred to the instrument as late as 1858 (Berlioz) and Geraert (1863) the keyed-bugle had by then had its day.

Four bugles. From left to right.
(i)   F(redrick) P(ace) c.1845. Single coil bugle.
(ii) Henry Keat, Matthias Rd, London, 1913. Copper bugle with unusual crook to F.
(iii) Henry Keat, buglet (c.1880), Popular in the early days of cycling.
(iv) H.Potter, London c.1900. Service bugle.

Mechanised bugles. From left to right:
(i)   F(redrick) P(ace). c.1845. Single coil bugle with crook to B♭. Tuneable at mouth-pipe, and unusually also tuneable rear bow.
(ii)   Keyed bugle. Astor & Co, 70 Cornhill, London. 1813. with 6 keys and a crook from C to B♭.
(iii)   H.Keat and Sons, 'Regent's Bugle' in E♭ with crook to C. A short-model slide trumpet but with deep, V-shaped conical mouthpiece.
(iv)   F.Besson, London. 3-valved flugelhorn.

The above bugles from the other side.

Five
The Cornetto and the Mock-Trumpet

Before leaving the subject of instruments related to the trumpet which rely upon finger holes or keys to fulfil their musical functions, it would seem timely to reflect backwards briefly upon two instruments whose repertoire is relevant to the trumpet although neither is made of metal.

The cornetto (French: cornet-à-bouquin, German: Zink, Spanish: Corneta, Italian: Cornetto) was a wooden instrument, normally with seven finger-holes with a cup shaped mouthpiece rather smaller than that of a trumpet. It was played throughout the 16th and 17th centuries in Europe, and was said to sound more like the human voice than any other instrument, for which reason it was useful for reinforcing the upper voices of cathedral choirs, whose lower sonorities were doubled by the sackbut (early trombone). Subsequently the grouping of cornettos and sackbuts was employed as a homogenous ensemble in its own right. In the past it was sometimes played by trumpeters, but nowadays invariably so, and this has led to widespread confusion of the manner and taste with which music originally written for the natural Baroque trumpet has been interpreted. The cornetto was more capable of virtuosic technical display than any other wind instrument, whereas the sheer dignity of the trumpet's tone lent itself to occasional simple ornamentation only. Players of the modern valved trumpet have invariably been unable to differentiate between the two styles to the detriment of much otherwise elegant repertoire.

Like many other instruments of Rennaisance times, the

cornetto spawned a whole family of smaller and larger instruments, the smallest being called a cornettino. It was generally pitched a fourth higher than its relative (early versions were sometimes a fifth higher) and suited only the very highest register; however by the 17th century the best players could master the highest notes on the cornetto itself in passages such as the 'Deposuit' in Claudio Monteverdi's *Vespers of the Blessed Virgin* (1610).

It should be pointed out that some scholars argue that this passage should sound a fourth lower, but that makes a subsequent passage for bass voice inordinately low.

The tenor cornetto was a fifth lower than the treble or standard instrument. It usually had an extra hole covered by a key, and to make it convenient to hold it was built with a double curve first to the right then to the left; this earned it the nickname of 'The Lizzard'. Even larger was the bass cornetto which is still known as the Serpent. Praetorius is said to have complained that the tenor cornetto sounded as unlovely as a bullock and Handel, equally disenchanted with the tone of the serpent commented sourly 'surely, this could not have been the sound that seduced Eve?'

But the treble cornetto in the hands of an accomplished

Renaissance cornetto (Christopher Monk) reproduction.

musician has an exceptional range of expression. A carving in Lincoln Cathedral dated about 1260 depicts an angel playing two cornetti at the same time in the manner of Pan. In Germany a straight treble cornetto without the customary curve to the right was used, as was the straight 'mute cornetto' with its softer, veiled tone quality. The finest early ensemble repertoire is that composed in Venice by Andrea Gabrieli (c. 1515–1586) and his nephew Giovanni (c. 1557–1612). Their style was imitated by composers across the Alps and in England cornettists were engaged as part of the Royal Musical Entourage. They were heard in various musical contexts in the 18th century such as Bach's *Funeral Cantata* (BWV 118), Handel's opera *Tamerlano* (1724) and Gluck's *Orfeo* (1762). In Rome they played in the Concerto Capitolino until 1789 and continued to play Tower Music in some German cities in the 19th century.

Some idea of the ornaments or 'divisions' improvised by players of the cornetto (and other treble instruments) in Italian music of Monteverdi's time may be gained by examining 'Canzona Passaggiata' in which Angelo Notari demonstrated how a simple melody should or could be decorated; the manuscript of this is in the British Library (Add. MS 31440). It was written after he settled in London c. 1610:

A second example, this time specifically for the cornetto, is given by Dalla Casa demonstrating his ornamentation of a melody by Lassus; this time the melody is on the lower line:

It will be noticed that both these examples of 'decorations' bear no resemblance to those heard on numerous recordings using modern 'piccolo' trumpets since the essence of cornetto playing is its extraordinary fluidity.

Fingering for the cornetto varies from one instrument to another on certain notes. Fundamentally it is not unlike the recorder in that during the process of manufacture the placing of the holes requires precision and different makers vary according to the internal bore of the instrument they choose. In principle once a hole is opened, those below it or towards the bell-end are left open unless one wishes to raise the note by only half a tone, in which case the next hole down remains closed (except for low G♯, high F♮). The upper notes are not consistent between one cornetto and another, and the player may need to experiment for themselves. The holes are numbered backbard from the bell and the seventh is underneath and therefore closed with the left hand thumb holes 7, 6, 5 and 4 employ the left hand and 1, 2 and 3 the right.

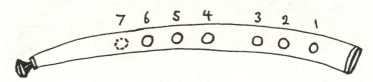

Open the following holes for the appropriate notes:

A detail is provided from Sandford's depiction of the Coronation cortège that processed at King James II's enthronement in London, showing a cornetto (he calls it wrongly 'shawm') between two sackbuts (which match James Talbot's description of a 'Flatt Trumpet') published two years after the event. The cornetto is being blown very typically out of the right corner of the player's mouth which suited the very small 'acorn' sized mouthpiece which was normally used. The association between sackbutts and Flatt Trumpets is interesting since a non-expert evidently perceived them as the same.

Officionados of the serpent may not regard it as a bass or contra-bass cornetto since it has smaller and larger versions which suggest that it had a family of its own, the largest of which is nicknamed the Annaconda. The serpent was first used in the 16th century; Handel employed it in the performance of his *Music for the Royal Fireworks* (1749) and in the 19th century it was written for by Rossini in *The Seige of Corinth*, by Mendelssohn in *St. Paul*, Wagner in *Rienzi* and Verdi in *The Sicilian Vespers*. It was the bass instrument in many village and church bands in England throughout the nineteenth century despite being described, by Cecil Forsyth, as having '. . . the appearance of a dishevelled drainpipe which was suffering internally.'

Another instrument with finger-holes used in the Baroque period is one which previous writers about the trumpet have overlooked. Like the 'Flatt Trumpet' which was discussed on earlier pages, the 'Mock Trumpet' should not be accorded more significance than it merits, but in some repertoire of the early 18th century it may explain the use of notes outside the harmonic series in music for which 'trumpet' has been specified. The fact that the musical examples given are taken from the fourth edition of the *Compleat Book for the Mock Trumpet* containing directions and tunes fitted to it, also 'very proper for ye Brazen Trumpet' shows that the instrument enjoyed some popularity. Walsh the publisher also advertised that the previous three editions, which presumably featured

From Sandford's depiction of James II's Coronation (1685)

other melodies, may also be purchased from him.

Like the cornetto, this instrument has seven finger-holes which cover the limited range from G at the bottom of the stave to just over an octave higher. It has a reed concealed beneath a piece of 'gilded leather' which produces the sound, the instrument is therefore a type of chalumeau or early clarinet which however is not capable of 'overblowing' into a second octave and its repertoire is severely restricted. But the melodies given to it are clearly those of the trumpet, and one can see how it developed by stages into the clarion-ette (small clarion) that ultimately was adopted as the 'new sound' of the late 18th and early 19th centuries. During the course of its evolution, the early clarinet continued to imitate the trumpet in concertos by Molter and Stamitz. This first example shows how it is deemed necessary on a short-tubed instrument to decorate the melodic line since the tone of the instrument (like the piccolo trumpet) does not exactly caress the ear:

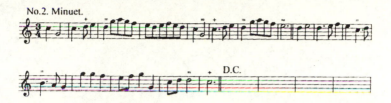

The book also contains 19 duets imitating trumpets:

Six
Valves

The valve is an 'instant' crook. Two operational systems from the earliest stages of development have superceded others and remain in use today; these are the piston and the rotating valve. In both of these, internal chambers divert the vibrating air through additional tubing which lowers the pitch of the note. The invention was announced in 1815 in the 'Allgemeine musikalische Zeitung' by the professional horn player, Heinrich Stoelzel. However, Friedrich Blühmel, with whom he had collaborated, insisted upon being party to the patent which was

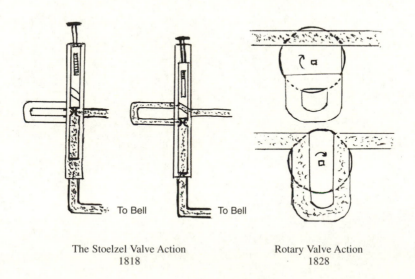

The Stoelzel Valve Action
1818

Rotary Valve Action
1828

issued jointly to them for ten years in 1818. The earliest designs had a square-sectioned valve, but Stoelzel soon decided that a tubular push valve was more efficient: this was adopted widely by English and French makers. The air enters the valves at right angles and turns 90° out of the bottom of it unless the valve is depressed, whereupon it travels around the additional tubing, back into the valve where it again turns downwards out of the bottom towards the bell. The rotary valve swivels at an angle of 90° so that its internal parallel tubes divert the air out into the extra tubing and back again.

Credit for the development of the rotary valve should go to Stoetzel's former collaborator Blühmel, whose request for a patent was rejected in 1828. At an early stage the rotating cylinder's two windways became quarter-circular so that the air column was less interrupted than by the sharp right angle of Stoetzel's narrow pistons.

In 1839 the French maker Pérìnet perfected the piston valve by inserting a third passageway into it whereby one of the ducts carries the air straight through by the shortest route back into the body of the trumpet or cornet. When the vale is pushed down the air is diverted around the extra tubing but the new third windway returns it to the point where it had previously travelled straight through towards the bell.

With minor refinements these two types of valve remain in use today. There were experiments with other systems such as the Viennese double-piston (1821) and Wieprech's 1835 'Berlin' piston which was short but broad enough to incorporate the quarter-circular windway of Blühmel's valve. In the 1820's other systems were invented independent of European influences by American manufacturers, and in 1838 J. Shaw introduced an English 'Disc' valve. This disc, upon which 2 semicircular bows can be rotated 90° to divert and return the air column through the additional tubing, is activated by a rod pushed by the fingers.

Early examples of piston trumpets have only two valves, one lowering the harmonic series by half a tone, the other by a whole tone and in combination by a tone and a half. Without crooks they are usually pitched in F and cover a full chromatic range from E below the stave upwards, omitting only the G♯ below the stave. When crooks are added the valve tubing needs

Two Cornopeans.
(i) Köhler, 35 Henrietta St, London (1839) with 3 'Shaw' disc valves.
(ii) Charles Pace, London (c.1850) with 3 valve-top covers, mouthpiece, shanks to B♭ and A and crooks to A♭, G and F. Apart from the bell-flares, these instruments have cylindrical tubing and no taper and are tecnically not cornets.

to be increased incrementally and the tuning will be found to be inconsistent in various registers and keys. The subsequent introduction of a third valve therefore not only delivered a low G♯ and extended the range chromatically downwards by nearly a further octave, but it gave alternative fingerings when problematic tuning was encountered. Furthermore crooking became unnecessary and trumpeters fell into the habit of transposing into whatever key was required of them.

Composers took some years to reconcile themselves to the new possibilities and potential liberation of the trumpet. The symphonies of Mendelssohn, Schumann and Brahms show a reluctance to abandon the trumpet's traditional role; it was left to the ever experimental and innovative composers of opera to exploit the new mechanisms although the process was demanding upon the players. The opening to the third act of Wagner's opera *Lohengrin* apparently requires five changes of crook in the very first line:

The impracticability of such changes demonstrates that players transposed as a matter of course from the earliest stages of the introduction of valved trumpets. The symphonies of Gustav Mahler often call for illogical changes of pitch with only moments between exposed solo passages, such as in Symphony No. 6:

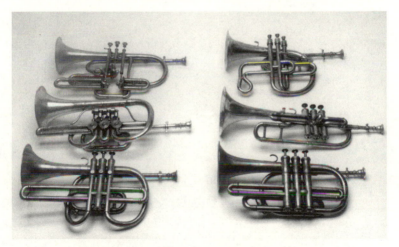

Six early cornets
(i)   Upper left; Köhler, cornopean, 1839. Pitched in B♭
(ii)   Upper right; C. Pace, cornopean, c.1850. Pitched in B♭
(iii)   Middle left; H. Dustin, London c.1860. B♭ cornopean with 3 rotary valves.
(iv)   Middle right; Distin, London 1855, E♭ Cornet.
(v)   Bottom left; A. Courtois for Julien & Co, London. c.1856. Unusual B♭ cornet with 2 Stölzel valves and one Périnet.
(vi)   F. Besson, 198 Euston Rd, London. B♭ Cornet. 1888.

These innovations occurred at a time when the boundaries of musical expression were being extended. Other orchestral instruments were also developing and the composer's tonal palette demanded ever more vivid colouration. Thus the trumpet became integrated into the general orchestral texture, sacrificing its former lofty, heroic stature which had formerly been the perquisite of its limitations.

Seven
Sibling Rivalries

According to the Bandmaster Wilhelm Wieprecht 'All Berlin players were against the invention' of the valve, and certainly in London the pre-eminence of Thomas Harper and his son both as players and as teachers, preserved the status of superiority enjoyed by the slide-trumpet until the final years of the 19th century. Writing in 1895, Algernon Rose asserts 'Although in our great orchestras 'trumpet' players may be advertised in the programmes, in nine cases out of ten these musicians perform their parts in an excellent manner, not on the trumpet but on the cornet . . . the fact is, musicians cannot get a living nowadays by playing the slide-trumpet.'

Mention has previously been made of the itinerant Italian trumpeter Alessandro Gambati and his brother who were engaged to play in the Orchestra of the King's Theatre, London in the late 1820's on their keyed-trumpets. After crossing the Atlantic in 1833 he established himself in New York where the reputation of the migrant English slide-trumpet player John Norton had been firmly established since his arrival in 1827. By this time Gambati was playing a trumpet pitched in either low G or F with two Stoelzel valves and on August 19th 1834 (staged by William Niblo, an impresario who owned New York's most popular Pleasure Garden at the corner of Broadway and Prince Street) strode up before Norton on the public stage 'arrayed in an enormous pair of military gloves of white deerskin' blowing on two trumpets and threw down a glove in challenge. Norton picked up the gauntlet and held it up before the audience in acceptance to thunderous applause

The Great "Trumpet Battle" in Niblo's Pleasure Gardens, New York, August 22nd and 25th 1834.
Top: John Thompson Norton (victor) with his slide-trumpet.
Bottom: Two-Valved trumpet as used by Alessandro Gambati.

which ensured that nearly four thousand people witnessed the contest on the following Friday evening.

Norton played in the best traditions of the English 'School', his choice repertoire being the great Handelian obligati. However, as is clear from his 'Preceptor for the trumpet', published before he left London, he was also adept at decorating a sentimental ballad in accordance with the current taste. Signor Gambati however specialised in the new Air Variée that was popular in Paris wherein 'his taste, fire and precision were much admired.' However 'he never was heard to ascend to the fifth line on any crook of the trumpet, but sported about below the line, ascending occasionally to the tonic on the third space, with infinite taste, but mediocre tone . . . When playing Handel's song 'The Trumpet Shall Sound' he actually was compelled to transpose the trumpet part a full octave below.'

Their distinctively different styles and instruments had been attracting partisans throughout that summer. Rivalry had been deliberately fostered by the New York Times who favoured Norton (flying the flag of St. George on the day of the contest) and the Evening Star who responded to the Times' initial provocation on July 31st in support of Gambati (raising the Italian Tricolour in reply). The choice of pieces raised problems since Gambati's variations on a theme from Rossini's *Cinderella* was not practicable on the slide-trumpet and Norton's suggestion of 'Let the Bright Seraphim' and 'The Trumpet Shall Sound' were beyond Gambati's range. Eventually it was settled that they should both play on the simple trumpet without valves, keys or slides (but they could hand-stop if they wished) and then they may play pieces and instruments of their own choice.

Interspersed between other musical offerings without trumpet solos, Gambati commenced with variations upon a march from Rossini's *Moses in Egypt* having been greeted with applause that 'echoed like thunder'. The 'Evening Star' subsequently reported that he did not play this as well as he could, probably because he was unaccustomed to the plain (natural) trumpet. They felt however that Norton's rendering of variations on 'Robin Adair' although tasteful and beautiful showed insufficient execution of rapid or difficult passages (upon the 'plain' trumpet). Gambati's second offering was probably the 'Willow Song' from *Othello* by Rossini. He played it with conviction upon his valved trumpet and received an 'encore'. Norton, bowing to public taste, abandoned Handel in favour of ornamenting a Scottish ballad, 'Logic O'Buchan', and 'The British Grenadiers'. The judges verdict was split and a rematch announced for the following Monday at which the trophy was awarded to Norton.

The victor returned to his job as director of music in the Chestnut Street Theatre, Philadelphia where he remained until his death in 1868; his trumpet is exhibited in the Smithsonian Institute, Washington DC (No. 237,756). Gambati's supporters claimed that he had driven Norton out of New York, but in fact Gambati moved to New Orleans where efforts were made to revive the 'Battle' in Dec. 1835, but came to nothing. Norton remained disdainful of his rival, claiming that he could play the famous Handel Arias 'on any plain (natural) trumpet better than Signor Gambati can upon the valve, keyed-, or slide-trumpet.' He further staked a thousand dollars that Gambati, 'could not execute them upon any trumpet!'

Norton's successor as professor of trumpet at the Royal Academy of Music in London was Thomas Harper (senior). His book of Instructions for the Trumpet published in 1835 was brought out in a second edition two years later. It is significant that he thought fit to add brief instructions also on playing not only the slide-trumpet (to which he gives 25 pages) but also the 'Russian' valve trumpet (with 2 pistons like Gambati's – this merits 5 pages) the piston cornet (which has 10 pages) the keyed-bugle (allotted another 10 pages) and finally a single page mentioning the cornetto as he knew it, which was a higher pitched cornet (in D with crooks down to B♭) upon which the first valve gave a semitone transposition of the harmonics and the second (middle) valve rendered them a whole tone lower. This obsolete instrument is rarely seen in collections; the semitone second valve is far more practical in the layout of any instrument from the maker's point of view, and like driving on the same side of the road, a standardised sequence of valves is more convenient.

In the preface to the tutor written by Harper's son (also called Thomas) he expressed regret that orchestral directors do not value the refined brilliance of a trumpet's tone, but are content to engage cornetists '. . . with more regard for economy than musical effect'. He explains in more detail, 'It is easier to produce the harmonic notes on the cornet than the trumpet (he is referring to the slide-trumpet); moreover, the flexibility induced by the pistons renders such florid passages facile upon the cornet, as have been supposed to be impracticable upon the trumpet. These facts make the former instrument attractive to many persons who wish to produce the loudest music with the least trouble, and who would never attempt to play on the latter because of its greater difficulties, notwithstanding it's purity and fineness of tone.'

Composers of theatrical entertainments welcomed the versatile cornet, and the many bands that were founded in mill and mining towns produced excellent musicians for them to employ. Within a short time municipal bandstands elevated the cornet to become a popular solo instrument, with an impressive repertoire of its own and arrangements of classical masterpieces. The best players therefore cultivated a florid technique. In only one area of music was it unable to advance and that was in the still popular performances of Handel's oratorios. It remained totally unthinkable that in the final pages of *Messiah* that a musician would come to the front of the orchestra with a cornet and bleat his way through the aria 'The Trumpet Shall Sound'. The public expected a proper trumpet at such moments and that is what they got until the surreptitious introduction of the long valved trumpet, bogusly called either the 'Bach' trumpet or the 'Handel' model. Upon close inspection some early versions have leadpipes that taper back from the first valve to receive a cornet mouthpiece!

The earliest trumpet of this type was developed in Berlin for the trumpeter Julius Kosleck in the 1870's. He used an almost conical mouthpiece to prevent the tone from becoming too shrill, since he regularly practised upon a military 'natural' trumpet and was aware of the results that it was capable of producing. He sought the accuracy of a valved instrument but was anxious to preserve the 'clarino' quality of clear 'vocal' playing. When he visited London in 1885 both audiences and critics were impressed, and his associates at that time, Walter Morrow and John Solomon, copied both his style and his instrument, one of which, by Silvani and Smith, pitched in A, belonged to Solomon and may be seen at the Bate Collection, Oxford. This created a new 'tradition' for Handel's works which eventually supplanted the old slide-trumpets; the long, straight trumpet, once shortened to D was used for *Messiah* and *Samson* well into the 1960's when it was still stirringly played by one of the author's teachers, Bernard Brown.

In 1845 a short trumpet in D was advertised for use in cavalry bands, and by the 1860's the Parisian maker Millereau was offering a sopranino trumpet in Piccolo B♭. Following this, various pitches of instrument could be specially made from high B♭ and G, through F and E♭ to D, which became the most popular although it was still at this time uncommon. In the first 30 years of the 20th century, many trumpets were equipped with a rotating cylinder that lowered the standard B♭ trumpet to A which saved the semitone transpositions which were required regularly, but also put Baroque music (sounding in D major at concert pitch) which had to be played in the key of E, into F, a key which lends itself to better trills and more secure intonation.

The B♭ trumpet which is universally used in bands, orchestras and studios nowadays, also encountered strong resistance from traditionalists. In the early years of the 20th century, the slide-trumpet which was pitched in F gave way to the 3 valved alto trumpet built at the same pitch; also capable of being adjusted with 'crooks', it related well to the French horn, conveniently for a considerable number of musicians who doubled on both instruments. Many trumpet mouthpieces of this period have rims that are uncomfortably sharp to modern players, but which suited those used to that of the horn. English proponents of the big F trumpet were Walter Morrow, John Solomon, Frank James and Edgar Sainsbury. Its lifespan in the orchestra may have been shorter than the extensive number of works written for it may suggest. Composers were used to scoring horns in F and it was not difficult for them to think of trumpets sounding an octave higher. The works of Elgar for example, such as the *Enigma Variations,* are extremely difficult for a modern player to pitch if he tries playing one of these old trumpets, (more so than upon a longer Baroque trumpet in D or C) mainly due to our lack of familiarity with hearing the resultant notes a fourth higher than they occur upon our 'normal' B♭ trumpets. There is no doubt that these players made life hard for themselves, even if unwittingly.

The London Symphony Orchestra in 1912 was rehearsing Richard Strauss' *Alpine Symphony* which takes the first trumpet in one exposed solo passage to sounding D above top C, and John Solomon, great player though he was, encountered such difficulty with the passage that enquiries were made whether there was a trumpeter in London capable of playing it with safety. Playing at the Lyceum Theatre at the time was a 22 year old pupil of Walter Morrow, who had never been comfortable on the larger trumpet. As a boy he had been taught the B♭ cornet in Liverpool, now he was proud to own and play a smart new B♭ Mahillon trumpet (displayed in the museum of the Royal College of Music, London alongside the slide-trumpet [converted from a c. 1720 Harris, Natural trumpet] played by Thomas Harper Senior). The young man whose name was Ernest Hall was summoned, and his incisive, accurate, bright playing gained him immediate admiration and membership of the orchestra. However, when the appointment was announced, John Solomon (then 56 years old) who had been a founding member of the orchestra addressed his colleagues with the reservation that this 'trumpettina' that Hall played was a passing 'fad' that would never catch on – the instrument was not a proper trumpet!

Solomon had in fact been engaged in the 1880's as both a trumpeter and cornetist at the Globe Theatre in London, and when Ernest Hall became principal trumpeter of the London

Symphony Orchestra, it was no great hardship for Solomon to play the B♭ trumpet also, which instrument he thereafter taught at the Royal Academy of Music. Both men lived to a great age. Solomon died in 1953 aged 96 and Hall lived until 1984 when we mourned his passing at the age of 94.

The trumpet in B♭ has remained the basic orchestral instrument in England ever since. It is very exciting to witness the present section of the London Symphony Orchestra performing symphonies by Mahler, all playing upon the B♭ trumpet. Maurice Murphy, it's outstanding principal trumpeter for the past 22 years has never had recourse to smaller trumpets in the course of his duties: this observation is not intended as a slight or criticism of the many outstanding players who choose otherwise. In France and the United States of America, whole sections play the instrument pitched in C, and many players keep an E♭ trumpet with them, whose smaller bore suits certain styles of music well, and which focuses some particular notes and musical passages to the satisfaction of many musical directors and recording producers.

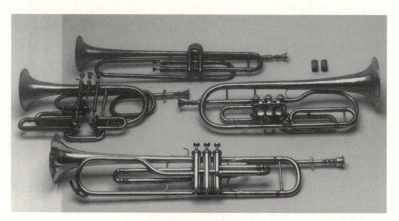

Four 'F' Trumpets.
(i)   Charles Pace, London (c.1840), with 2 Stoelzel valves (and valve-caps)
(ii)   Middle left; Köhler. 1839 with `Shaw disc valves (cornopean, or short-stopped-trumpet, crooked to F)
(iii)   Middle right; Joseph Lidle, Brno (c.1900) rotary valves.
(iv)   W. Brown & Sons, 2 Tracey St, London. (c.1905)

The use of different sizes of trumpet was perfected to a fine art by the late John Wilbraham who would appear in the studio or concert hall with as many as six different trumpets. He would sometimes pick one up just to cover a few bars and then transfer to another; he never mispitched and knew exactly which trumpet he preferred for every entry in the entire symphonic repertoire. In the film studio he would cast his eye quickly over each successive cue and in seconds select the trumpet which best suited him. He transposed at sight faultlessly whatever music was put before him upon whatever pitch of trumpet he had in his hand. Those of us who sat beside him were always amazed at the results which did not sound like 'toy' trumpets even when 'piccolo' instruments in high B♭, A and G were used – the latter was a great favourite of his. The task of playing second trumpet to him was one that demanded great musicianship and adaptability, so credit must be given to his long-time second trumpet Iaan Wilson who accomplished this (unusually in England) upon a trumpet in C for most of the time.

The author's 'everyday' trumpets.
(i)   Top: Vincent Bach (USA) B♭ trumpet. 1982
(ii)   Middle left: H. Selmer, Paris. 1967. piccolo B♭/A
(iii)   Middle right: H. Selmer, Paris, 1970. E♭/D trumpet
(iv)   Bottom; H. Selmer, Paris, 1982. Piccolo B♭/A (straightened by the author)

Four early 20th Century B♭ trumpets.
(i)   Left: King 'Liberty' B♭ trumpet. 1921, Cleveland USA.
(ii) Second from left: W. Brown & Sons, Kennington, London, c. 1930 B♭ trumpet
with rotary change to A.
(iii) Anon. (German) c. 1956. 3 Rotary valves
(iv) Below it: Dismantled 'Aida' trumpet by W. Brown and Sons. c.1908. This has
(not shown) changeable valve slides and tuning pieces to play in E♭, D, B♭, A and A♭

Eight
Recent Developments

Various changes have effected the equipment that trumpet players use in the twenty-first century; the widespread availability
of instruments in various pitches have conditioned listeners to
accept a broad spectrum of tonal quality, and to some extent
their critical faculties have been blunted in the process.
Baroque music is heard both upon short (26 inches or 66 cm)
piccolo trumpets and vented (so-called) Baroque-style trumpets
of nearly 8 feet (294 cm). In a bizarre juxtaposition of artistic
logic, a regrettably increasing number of players incline to
reproduce qualities of the former upon the latter, encouraged by
the ignorance and lack of imagination of those who employ
them – the majority of 'Early Music' recordings of religious
choral music for example pay lip service to using reproductions
of 'period' instruments, but engage a chorus composed of
aspiring Grand Opera singers to represent choirboys!.

This anomaly must also be blamed on the altered perceptions
of sound quality that has evolved in response to the recent
developments in electronic gadgetry that have stimulated the
record industry – providing a substantial part of musicians'
incomes in the process. Instrument designers have attempted to
keep pace with these changes, and with the demands of novel
approaches to the subject of acoustics adopted by the architects
of new concert halls.

The greatest change however is one of musical style since the
advent of jazz. The fundamental element of individual creativ-
ity and spontaneous expression which is the essence of musical
improvisation is well attuned to popular culture. The rigorous

disciplines of élitist art forms remained dismissive in their attitude and shunned these new influences, but the greatest exponents became household names whose repuations linger in our memories – Louis Armstrong, Bix Beiderbeck and Miles Davis for example.

In the hands of such players, the trumpet (and cornet) regained a prominent rôle. The cornet had featured as a virtuosic solo instrument in the late Victorian and Edwardian music-halls, almost as a curiosity and for the first time female players appear on concert bills including 'All Ladies Orchestras'. Anna Teresa Berger (1853–1925) had toured the American Vaudeville circuit as an infant prodigy; in 1889 she featured nightly in the Covent Garden promenade concerts between August 17th and September 28th and intermittently thereafter until November 4th. Her portrait graced the front cover of 'The Illustrated Sporting and Dramatic News' (October 26th 1889), London. Some of her contemporary male soloist colleagues boasted a chromatic register of four octaves

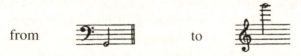

which few achieve a century later!

Band cornets were cheaper and more readily available in the early years of the 20th century, and they were used in the earliest stages of the embryonic jazz bands. In the 1920's and 1930's the popular dance bands generally employed trumpets and as these swelled to form the 'Big Bands' of the 1940's and 1950's trumpet sections allocated specific registers to their members ('Screamer', 'Lead', 'Hot'-improviser, and 'down the line' – many fulfilled several of these functions) developing the instincts of 'Swing' whereby collective careful listening to other musicians returned artistic responsibility to the players from the hands of the 'Maestro' conductor.

Subsequently the music for 'Light Entertainment' shows, films, television and advertisements have required stylistic versatility from professional musicians who, from economic necessity, have to adapt to various idioms which inevitably eventually fuse to transform or ostracise earlier practices or mannerisms; thus died the string 'portamento', gut strings, the wooden flute and the crisp small-bore brass.

There has also been a trend, whether conscious or not, (probably brought about by the increasing use of 'close' microphones) to eliminate the overtones from the sound of all instruments of the brass family. If one listens to the famous old children's favourite 'Tubby the Tuba' as recorded over sixty years ago by Danny Kaye, the sound of the tuba playing almost seems on the point of 'breaking up' and such a performance would never pass the studio door now. The B♭ bass tuba is rarely heard at all today since we have become accustomed to the 'clean' sound of the shorter instrument in F. Likewise, much recorded French horn playing has abandoned the conventional instrument pitched in F for one sounding a fourth higher in B♭.

The bass trombone in G (or F) has been substituted by a B♭ one with 'plugs' or valves to engage additional tubing when required, and in many countries, apart from England and Russia, trumpets in C are frequently used to give a brighter, more focused sound. At the same time all these instruments use tubing of wider bore, and have bell flares much more pronounced than those used earlier. The latter undoubtedly give greater security, especially when loud playing is required, but the tone has deliberately broadened – which has been deemed desirable – giving an evenness of sound throughout the range, which critics say makes the horn sound like a euphonium, the tuba like a baritone and the trumpet indiscernible from the cornet, many models of which are equipped with a mouthpiece-cup exactly similar to that of a trumpet. Certainly there are some trumpets on the market now that taper throughout their entire length (except for the few inches of the valve section) which but for a cupped mouthpiece, as opposed to a conical one, are cornets in all but name.

Little has changed since Perinet perfected the valves, the

layout having the first valve (nearest the player) lowering the harmonics by a whole tone, the second or middle valve being half the length and delivering a semitone with the third valve lowering the pitch by a tone and a half. Most quality instruments have adjustable sleeves on the first and third valves to perfect intonation; these are operated either by finger-rings or levers. Many smaller trumpets in E♭, F, G, and high (piccolo) B♭ have a fourth valve to lower the pitch by a fourth. This completes a theoretical lower octave, and certainly extends the instrument's range downwards, also providing useful alternative fingering.

Conservatories in France and the United States have encouraged a comprehensive study of trumpeting in all types and styles of music, but in Germany and Britain it is only recently that courses have embraced disciplines other than 'Classical'. This sensible approach permits students to graduate with not only a fuller understanding but with a wider scope of opportunities with which they may begin earning their livelihood. There are also opportunities to play brass instruments in the environment of chamber music, in brass quintets and ensembles of anything up to the size of a symphonic brass and percussion section. The quality of some of this repertoire is extremely high, therefore it is possible to devise programmes that range from medieval to contemporary music that will provide audiences with a varied and entertaining experience. It is worth cultivating the use of different sounds, especially those that rest the ear from the wearing sound of high trumpets. Particularly useful is the flugel-horn or, as it is more aptly described in France, the bugle with valves. This has the shape and dimensions of the old keyed-bugle but utilises three pistons, or in Germany, Austria and Italy, rotary valves. Due to its widely expanding bell and deep conical mouthpiece, it produces a mellow, lyrical tone that lends itself to great expressiveness.

Nine
Mutes

The trumpet was the earliest wind instrument to use a mute, but like other accessories they are invariably missing from their parent instrument in historic collections. This is regrettable since subsequent observers give conflicting and sometimes misleading commentaries on the subject. The largest collection of antique trumpet mutes is held in the music department of the National Museum in Prague where 18 specimens are preserved, many in good condition considering their age; however, what age that is has not been ascertained for any of them, even though the name 'Vamberk' is inscribed upon three. Those players who have conducted research and practical experimentation have inserted them into the bells of 18th century trumpets (or reproductions thereof) to find that the pitch is raised by half a tone in contradiction of earlier writers who all maintained that the pitch rose a whole tone upon the trumpet's harmonics once the mute was inserted. However the musical deployment of this early type of mute occurs much more frequently in 17th century compositions, and the author has found that these mutes inserted into the broader 'Renaissance' style bells of 17th century trumpets do indeed raise the pitch by nearly a whole tone, which may account for instruments also being supplied as a matter of course with a crook that again lowers the pitch by a whole tone. This would render muted and unmuted trumpets compatible in consort, which is what Monteverdi specifies for performing the 'Toccata' to his opera *L'Orfeo* – a clarino with three muted trumpets (see music ex.1, p.16). It will be noticed that the lowest part ('basso') remains unmuted;

practical experiments reveal that this note (the second harmonic) does not speak freely with a mute inserted, and like all innovative composers Monteverdi was aware of what was, and what was not playable by his performers. This also gives further evidence that 'clarino' playing was restrained in character unlike the more martial sounds of the Quinta, Alto and Vulgano registers.

These early mutes are gracefully carved of wood. They vary in shape, length and width but the principles of their construction is consistent. The main bowl, whose exterior surface holds the mute in the trumpet bell, is about 0.9 inches in diameter (2.28 cm) sinking to a depth of 1.2 inches (3.05 cm) whereafter it terminates in a hemispherical internal cup of 0.45 inches (1.14 cm) depth. The sound then passed through a narrow cylindrical throat from 0.18 inches (0.4 cm) to 0.4 inches (1 cm) in diameter and 2.6 inches (6.6 cm) in length, into a terminal 'bell' that remarkably resembles a trumpet mouthpiece 0.69 inches (1.75 cm) in diameter. The throat section is always decorated with carved rings which enable the player to grasp the mute inside the trumpet and remove it.

Such a mute is illustrated in Martin Mersenne's 1635 treatise *Harmonicorum libri XII* and repeated in his 1636 *Harmonie Universelle* explaining also '. . . it makes the sound softer and more dispersed, or weaker because, obviously, it makes the hollow of the bell more narrow, since the breath exits only through the hollow of the tubule.'

Three of the Prague mutes are designed differently. Instead of the terminal mouthpiece-like bell, they are reversible with a choice of main bowls that give slightly different pitches. Atenburg describes a third type of mute, which is even more sophisticated:

'There are different kinds. The first is equally narrow at both ends, the second is almost like a bell or a shawm at one of its ends, and the third kind has the shape of an oboe or clarinet. At the bottom, several small wooden rings can be inserted or removed at will, whereby the sound can be made louder or softer.' He also usefully continues: 'The mute is properly used 1) when an army wishes to break camp silently, so that the enemy will not be aware. 2) at funerals and burials. 3) To develop a good enduring embouchure through daily practice. 4) To keep the tone from being so screeching. 5) To bring into tune with music in many keys therewith.'

The earliest reference to the use of muted trumpets in funeral ceremonies dates from 1512 in the biography of Piero di Cosimo. There is further abundant evidence that during the course of the 16th and 17th centuries, muted or 'closed' trumpets were employed to accompany the corpse and mourners on foot, whilst towards the front of the column of attendants '. . . came riding a Trumpett in Livery or Colours of the House, sounding and denouncing war.' Two pairs or groups of trumpeters in mourning livery followed 'sounding a Mort Sound' in alternation – one group played whilst the other rested. At the graveside mutes were evidently removed when the coffin was interred, as the 'Sound of Open trumpets' symbolised that 'all the people craved at God a happy resurrection of his Soul'. The significance of 'open' trumpets being mentioned is that they must have been 'closed' or muted previously for the observation to have been made at all.

An extensive study of the use of the trumpet in British funerals of the 17th century by Alexander McGrattan may be found in the Historic Brass Society Journal Vol. 7 (1995). He provides a number of relevant pictures and prints, none of which appear to show any noticable apparatus emanating from trumpet bells. However, if those mutes used in Britain resembled those seen in Prague, they would have travelled at least 5 inches (12.7 cm) up the trumpet bell (thereby raising the pitch by the proscribed whole tone) and their overall length being 4.5 inches (11.43 cm) they would not have been visible.

It is significant that the first composition in which the trumpet was introduced into a string ensemble, the Sonata Op. 35 No. 10 by Maurizio Cazzati (1665) raises the pitch from C to D by use of a mute. Presumably, it was expected that the 'open' trumpet would be too loud, but as we know, such control was achieved that the instrument was immediately integrated into the embryonic orchestra.

During the 18th century the trumpet seems to have been accepted for what it was, and mutes came to be used for effect rather than as a standard piece of equipment. By 1780 Mozart was writing from Munich to his father about the need to borrow mutes from the Stadtpfeifer of Salzburg for use in his opera *Idomineo* indicating that Munich players no longer saw fit to own them. The transposing potential of the mute became redundant once mechanised instruments were introduced. A few examples exist of wooden mutes from the 19th century, when cork was fashioned to permit the sound to pass outside the wooden bowl which was now sealed, between the mute and the wall of the trumpet bell. The entire unit was often covered in leather which afforded a good grip upon metal surfaces, also rendering the process of insertion soundless.

The use of three strips of cork glued to the narrow end of the mute persisted throughout the twentieth century. The standard 'straight' mutes are now manufactured in a variety of materials each of which respond differently; the choice is made according to personal taste although occasionally composers or directors may specify one particular type. Most players equip themselves with one that can reduce the tone to a 'distant' whisper and another (usually metal) that intensifies the tone in fortissimo for passages such as are found in Stravinsky's *Petroushka*. Earlier in the century softer sounds were obtained by wooden, cardboard and papier-mâché, but nowadays plastic produces excellent results also. The metallic mutes are generally manufactured in aluminium which is light and robust and which also resonates well: some manufacturers offer the option of a copper base to the straight mute which gives a slightly less brittle timbre. It is desirable for players in orchestras and bands of all types that the whole section should play matching mutes to obtain a homogenous sound together.

It is important to give regard to the condition of the corks from time to time, since once they wear thin with use, the mute travels too far into the trumpet bell rendering the pitch noticably sharper than when unmuted. If corks are fitted that are too wide, the aperture on the mute (which varies from 0.6 inches (1.5 cm) to 0.8 inches (2 cm)) is held in the wrong part of the bell and the sound becomes unfocused and fuzzy.

Mainly under the influence of jazz musicians a whole range of different sounds are available through the deployment of various mutes. The cup mute has the same shape as a straight mute, but over the broad end an additional bowl catches the air as it travels out of the gap between the mute's side and the trumpet bell, reducing the volume and resonance to produce a very 'sweet' tone. Recently a cup has been devised that is adjustable along the main body of the mute, which ingeniously permits the player to vary the degree of 'sweetness' and volume: this cup is also removable leaving a plain 'straight' mute underneath. Some makers have a removable cup that is also usable as a 'plunger' mute. Jazz musicians have recourse to this effect which is arresting to the ear and eye alike – many choose in fact to avail themselves of a domestic sink plunger which being some 4¾ inches wide (12.06 cm) exactly covers a trumpet bell so that with dexterity, remarkable results can be obtained since the bell can be fully or half covered, or played open; also the bell can be opened or closed in the course of playing a single note.

An effect not dissimilar can be achieved by cupping the left hand over the small apperture at the end of a 'Harmon' mute. This is made rather differently because a cork surrounds the narrow end to hold it firmly in the instrument, but the bowl follows the contour of the bell at the termination of which a further bowl some 2 inches (5.08 cm) in depth is attached in which is housed a 4 inch (10.16 cm) tube with a small 1.7 inches (4.32 cm) addition 'bell' at its end. This tube extends and retracts inside the Harmon mute or can be removed altogether, each time an adjustment is made, the sound is altered. However the most distinctive feature of this mute is that the hand can reach down over the small bell on the central tube to produce the comical 'Wa-Wa' effect that gives this mute its nickname.

A particularly pleasing effect is derived from a Bucket-mute which normally clips over the rim of the trumpet's bell. It has the shape of an inverted canister 4 inches (10.16 cm) deep which stands a further inch (2.54 cm) clear of the bell. Cotton wool is packed inside it to deaden the sound which emerges pleasantly mellow. An alternative design, that saves the bell rim from possible scratching, holds the bucket on three legs internally in the bell with corks.

One final mute, of which most players avail themselves, is the 'Practice' mute which can be invaluable in the confines of an hotel room, or backstage in a theatre when practice or 'warming-up' is necessary to the trumpeter but unwelcome to all others. Electronic gadgetry has recently produced a system whereby earphones enable the player to experience the

Ten mutes for trumpets of different eras.
(i)   Upper left: Wooden Baroque-period mute (reproduction)
(ii)   Upper centre: Slide-trumpet mute (c.1840). Wood covered in leather.
(iii)   Upper right: Slide-trumpet mute (c.1880). Wood with 3 corks.
(iv)   Middle left: Fibre (soft) mute with corks c.1920.
(v)   Middle, second from left: Modern metal mute with copper base and 3 corks by Tom Crown, USA.
(vi)   Middle, second from right: Modern piccolo trumpet metal mute by Dennis Wick, London.
(vii)   Middle extreme right: Modern adjustable cup-mute for B♭ trumpet by Dennis Wick, London.
(viii)   Bottom left: Harmon or 'wa-wa' mute.
(ix)   Bottom middle: Practice mute.
(x)   Bottom right: 'Bucket' mute.

sensation of playing in an open hall whilst giving an onlooker the impression that the musician is miming. Alternatively a conventional straight mute can be corked like a harmon mute to divert the air into it, but the sound can be released only through one (or two) very small holes 0.18 inches (4 cm) in diameter which is inaudible in an adjacent room.

In the Victorian and Edwardian music halls audiences were held spellbound by the simple gimmickry of an 'Echo-Cornet'. This has a fourth valve operated by the forefinger of the left hand which transmits the sound away from the main bell into an echo-chamber instead; this can also be done instantaneously to great effect.

Cornets can accept the same mutes as the trumpet and for 'plunger' and 'Wa-Wa' manipulations are much more convenient for those with shorter arms (like the author!). These mutes are also available in smaller sizes for 'piccolo' trumpets.

Two unusual cornets.
(i)   Left: A. Turtle, Manchester. 1912. A 'Pocket' or 'Preacher's' cornet in B♭. Used by streetcorner evangelists to lead hymn-singing.
(ii) Right: An 'Echo' cornet which has a fourth valve beside the first valve, operated by the left hand forefinger it diverts the notes into an 'instant' mute on the left side of the cornet. This is tuneable and produces a very entertaining effect. Dated 1889.

Ten
The Vented 'Baroque-Style' Trumpet

As part of the course at all institutions of advanced musical study in Britain, trumpet students are encouraged to learn an instrument that has come to be referred to as the 'Baroque' trumpet or even (quite incorrectly) as the 'Natural' trumpet. It is, as readers should now be fully aware, not the instrument known to Bach and Handel in anything but external appearance, for instead of being held in one hand (which leaves the chest and rib cage free to support the air column necessary to play it well) it is held like a modern trumpet or cornet in the left hand and requires the fingers of the right hand to cover anti-nodal vent-holes. This instrument has become institutionalised as an acceptable compromise because audiences and conductors cannot or will not accept the 'natural' untempered intonation of a real unvented trumpet – any more than Charles Burney could in 1784 (see keyed and 'harmonic' trumpet).

The way these holes work can be understood by examining how harmonics are produced from a tube. If, as on a hunting horn, the lips cause the air inside it to vibrate, it will at some point be found that the vibrations become focused and a clear note produced. This happens because the vibrations have found their 'fundamental' pulse. This occurs upon any length of tubing, the pitch of the note being identified by its length. If the lip is caused to vibrate faster, the pulses eventually settle on a second harmonic determined by the vibrations halving themselves and focusing upon a note an octave higher; the next harmonic a fifth higher still is created by the pulses quartering themselves. With successive fractions the harmonics progressively ascend:

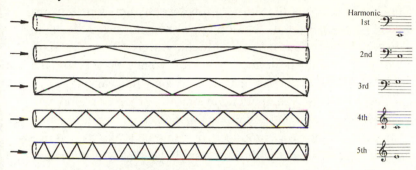

Each place at which the sound waves rebound from the walls of the tubing is called a nodal point.

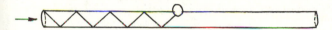

A hole perforating the tubing at such a point will cause the vibration of the pulses to cease, and will have the effect of halving the vibrating air column. Even though the same sounding note is being produced its quality is affected because it is resonating with only half its overtones.

For this reason connoisseurs remark that our compromising finger hole systems deliver a 'modern' sound (especially when using modern mouthpieces) on equipment that merely tries to look 'old'. Certainly the results are idealistic and sanitised compared with genuine attempts to recreate performances of the past, but they lack that 'on the edge' sensation which is particularly exciting; it is rather in the nature of a 'Hollywood' perception of performance practice. As the author has remarked before, how is it that cowboys after dusty hours in the sweating heat of the prairies still manage to arrive at journey's end with pristine creased shirts ready for the last scene of the film?

The vented trumpet at least makes us pause to consider that there may be different approaches to interpreting music of particular periods, and that perhaps early Baroque music does not have to sound like a Victorian 'Air-Varìee'. From the practical viewpoint the study of this recently developed instrument strengthens the developing embouchure and helps to dispel the apprehension of harmonics higher than the sixth which is ingrained in the minds of young players by the repertoire and text books of their early playing years.

There are two systems generally in use whose development must be credited to Otto Steinkopf and Michael Laird. The first 'modern clarino' was produced by Helmut Finke as a thrice coiled Jäger-Trumpet with three vent holes that were placed as follows:

1) Covered by the little finger of the right hand was a hole exactly half way between the mouthpiece and bell of the instrument effectively halving the length of the vibrating air column. This theoretically raises the entire harmonic series by an octave:

but in practice gives a weak or 'fuzzy' quality to the low 'G' (3rd harmonic).

2) The first or index finger of the right hand covered a hole lowering this octave transposition by a semitone, being placed slightly further towards the bell end of the trumpet. In practice this vent was only acceptably serviceable upon the notes B♮, E♭, F♯ high B♮ and high C♯ when required:

3) A third vent placed considerably further towards the bell, almost half way between the bell and the octave hole (but by virtue of the coiled design conveniently placed under the

right hand thumb) raised the harmonic series by a perfect fourth:

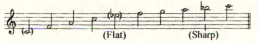

This gave a range of fingerings that covered most notes required in the trumpet parts of Bach and earlier Germanic and Moravian composers.

Noticeably missing are the low D, F♯ and G♯ required in the slide-trumpet parts of Bach's chorales, and the D♮ in the middle of the stave being only obtainable with 'natural' or closed fingering had a markedly different quality to the C and E on either side of it. Impressive results were produced by Walter Holy in Cologne with whom Michael Laird undertook a course of study. Upon returning to London he devised in his own workshop a layout engaging these same principles but upon a more conventional trumpet shape. He modestly never claimed credit for his contribution to a system that has been adopted by several German and Swiss makers ever since.

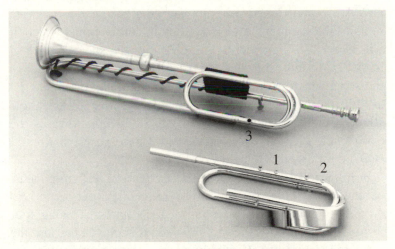

Trumpet with 3 venting holes, by Egger of Basle (2001)

One of the problems that came to light with this system was that of 'fine' tuning to orchestral pitch. The conventional extension or reduction of length at the mouthpiece end slightly, but sometimes critically, alters the accoustical geometry whereupon the vents fail to coincide with the precise nodal points and both tone and intonation are impaired. This could have been, but was not rectified to some extent by enlargement of the vents from 0.16 inches (0.4 cm) and 0.24 inches (0.6 cm) respectively of the octave and thumbholes to 0.2 inches (0.5 cm) and 0.36 inches (0.91 cm). Scientific advice always insists upon keeping vent holes small if possible, but the author has found that a purer, cleaner sound is produced through a larger hole and certain of the notes can be better bent or 'lipped' in tune.

The uneven and insecure tone of the middle-of-the-stave 'D' was rectified by Michael Laird's subsequent development of a four hole trumpet that returned the instrument to its simple historical oval shape and moved the thumb vent by between 5 and 6 inches (12.7 cm and 15.25 cm) depending upon the required pitch backwards from the octave hole towards the bell. This lowers the harmonics produced upon the octave vent by a whole tone theoretically, but in practice gives B♭ in the middle of the stave, D♮ above it (which is slightly flat) F♮ on the top line, also A♭, B♭ and C♮ above it. Between the two vents discussed remains the semitone vent covered by the index finger which, it will be recalled, gives B♮ in the middle of the stave, E♭, F♯ and high B♮. Missing from this almost complete scale is A♮ above the stave which is flat as a natural harmonic, and remains flat as the 7th harmonic of the index finger vent. An additional hole slightly higher in pitch and one inch (2.54 cm) towards the octave hole gives an excellent A♮ and if necessary a sharper E♭ (D♯) a diminished fifth below.

Both these systems are criticised by purists, and proponents of the three hole system have frequently been heard to pronounce it as being more 'authentic' than that using four vents. More serious is the way in which it is played because the vents fail to respond effectively when a large bowled Baroque

A modern, vented 'Baroque-Style' trumpet (made by the author c.1985) Four finger-holes may be discerned on the lower yard, towards the rear.

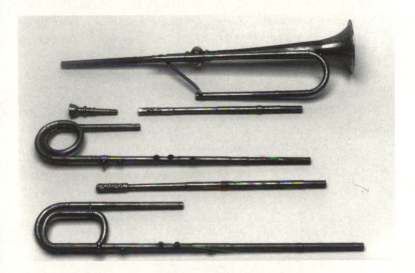

A vented trumpet dismantled. Segments from the top:
(i)   Bell section with forward 'Bow' soldered to it
(ii)   Mouthpiece and leadpipe in D
(iii)   Rear bow (crook) and fingerholes in D
(iv)   Leadpipe in C
(v)   Rear bow (crook) and fingerholes in C.

mouthpiece is used; that supplied is invariably as shallow as that used upon a modern trumpet, even if it bears the external appearance of an antique mouthpiece.

One drawback of these vented trumpets entering the academic curriculum, is that students will inevitably proceed directly from playing through Mahler symphonies or brass ensembles into their Baroque music tutorials and thereafter into the 'Big Band' so that all these sounds and styles fuse into a bizarre musical 'gel' from which habits both good and bad may be derived.

Finding material to practise however is not a problem, and rehearsing together in pairs or sections to cover the extensive output of Bach, Handel and Purcell both trains the ear and strengthens the lip. It is very important to alternate parts because although the florid clarino music may seem more glamorous, it is the lower parts, with large leaping intervals and awkward jumps that the young player is most likely going to be required to play when he first enters the profession. An extensive choice of makers now place their wares at our disposal. It is advisable to select a trumpet that plays well in all keys and in all pitches (Baroque A = 415, Classical A = 430 and Modern A = 440) because there is likely to be continued if not increased demand for less harsh and abrasive playing in interpretations of 'classical' and 'romantic' music in the future.

Eleven
The Mouthpiece

There can be no doubt that the most important item of a trumpet player's equipment is the mouthpiece. Upon it depends the ease and accuracy with which the notes are produced, the control of their intonation and the quality of their sound. As Thomas Harper Junior succinctly puts it 'with a good mouthpiece it is possible to play upon a badly constructed instrument; but with a badly proportioned mouthpiece it is impossible to play in tune, or with any degree of certainty, upon the best of instruments.' His father had advocated the use of the same mouthpiece in all the instruments that he played (slide-trumpet, keyed-bugle, valved F-trumpet and cornet) and nowadays one does find players using the same for trumpet, flugelhorn and piccolo trumpet even though, in the author's opinion, this defies some of the laws of physics and eliminates those charming differences in tonal character that lend these various instruments their individuality.

The point of contact between the player's lips and the body of the trumpet is the rim of the mouthpiece, and this is a personal matter of choice, although one should be aware of the ill effects of a hasty or bad selection since that which initially feels wonderful may not be suitable after a few days trial. John Hyde in his 1799 'Preceptor' writes: 'Choose a proper mouthpiece, large or small proportional to the thickness of the lips . . .' Altenburg goes into more detail 'A rim which is too wide hinders the embouchure somewhat, in that it reduces the freedom of the lips and covers them too much. A rim which is too narrow, on the other hand, does not promote an accurate or enduring embouchure and tires the lip in a short time'.

Two hundred years later we can find little to add to these wise words. Also with regard to the mouthpiece cup or 'bowl' Altenburg summarises that it 'contributes much to the loudness and softness of the sound, according to whether it is deep or shallow, wide or narrow. With a deep, wide mouthpiece one can play louder providing good service in the field pieces or principal parts. On the other hand a cup which is too shallow and narrow would not produce the proper loudness'.

He continues, of the throat or inside opening of the mouthpiece 'according to its relative narrowness or width [it] influences the comparative highness and lowness of the sound. Since the air which is driven into a small opening remains compact, it is thus strong enough on account of its elasticity, to set the resonant body into vibration at once and make it sound. On the other hand, expanding into a wider opening with less strength and pressure, it will then produce only the low tones.'

The problem confronting a modern player is that he or she is expected to perform equally well upon the regular trumpet, the cornet, flugelhorn, piccolo trumpet and probably the vented Baroque-style trumpet also. Each of these should be played upon a different mouthpiece that is designed for each particular instrument, the flugelhorn and cornet especially benefiting from a deep conical cup and that of the piccolo trumpet possibly being shallow to facilitate the production of its higher notes (and to keep them well in tune). Such a shallow mouthpiece can help in playing the upper register of the regular trumpet, but the tone tends to become shrill, moreover in the middle and low registers the sound becomes thin and lifeless. The player needs to be fully aware of the prerequisites of a good mouthpiece before making their selection even though the criteria have changed little since Altenburg's day.

The rim will determine not only the efficiency of the lips' vibrations, but the rate at which the muscles tire and therefore the player's endurance. One that is too thin digs into the flesh of the lips and will reduce the flow of blood to the delicate tissues and muscles surrounding the embouchure. This blood is transporting from the heart and lungs the oxygen that refreshes and energises the muscles, and if it's supply is cut off the muscles will weaken causing the sensation of 'lip go-ing'. This also happens when undue force or pressure is applied in the higher notes or when a young player first ascends to the top of the stave. A wider rim, especially if its edges are smoothly curved, spreads the area of contact over a greater area of facial tissue, and once the muscles have developed will spread the circumference of supporting muscles outwards, employing those at the side of the face, under the eyes, back towards the ears and all around the chin. These will be required in the development of range and endurance, and when strong should alleviate the misguided urge to increase pressure upon the lips either for high notes or in loud passages.

The circumference of the rim may depend upon the depth of the cup, since to produce a true trumpet tone it needs to be in the shape of a hemispherical bowl at the apex of which the air passes through the throat of the mouthpiece into the trumpet. In this cavity the character and quality of the sound is determined. The benefits and limitations of insufficient depth of this cup have been mentioned previously and are not infrequently encountered in players who become preoccupied or obsessed with the ambition of producing high notes from the instrument. Equally, there are those who hope to play with a fuller or 'fatter' sound (sometimes misleadingly thought to be 'bigger') by employing a wider or deeper cupped mouthpiece than really suits them. In this case the player has the physical sensation of massive volume, but like using a trumpet of very wide bore tubing, or widely flaring bell, the sensation is not matched by the end product, and at a short distance the sound is disappointingly weak. Often the listener receives the impression that the instrument is not being fully filled with tone – the reverse of what had been anticipated by the player. It should be mentioned in passing that the deep-bowled mouthpiece produces a less incisive attack or front to each note and when microphones are placed near to the trumpet bell, a comparatively shallow 'bright' production transmits more directly onto an audio tape or across the airwaves, it also focuses the intonation very positively whereas a deep mouthpiece can (or has to) be adjusted all the time.

The emission of sound is also effected by the throat of a mouthpiece, both with regard to the ease with which music is produced in varous registers, and again in control of tuning. If the apperture is too small and narrow, a great deal of resistance to the air column is experienced, on the other hand, if the hole is very wide, there is insufficient resistance and the airflow may be too free. Most players strike a compromise, but more than a few have ruined a good mouthpiece by opening it too much with a Reamer – the author being no exception! As with the rim and cup, individual requirements will influence choice – the lead trumpeter in a Big Band and the performer of second trumpet parts of a Mozart opera are not necessarily looking for the same qualities although the versatility required of a modern player demand a degree of compromise.

For some the solution is a mouthpiece that dismantles into three component sections that may be mixed and reassembled at will; these screw into one another so that a choice of rims, cups and mouthpiece stems (which contain the throat and backbore) may be combined to suit particular circumstances and musical requirements.

This enables the trumpeter to retain an especially favourite or comfortable rim, with shallow piccolo trumpet bowls and deep flugelhorn ones; the one drawback is that the adjustment takes time and an immediate switch, which is sometimes required, cannot be effected. It takes confidence and practice to change from one mouthpiece to a completely different one, but many players do this as a matter of course and, without difficulty.

A word of warning may be timely since one sees only too frequently excellent players becoming neurotic about mouthpieces during their careers. One naturally encounters problematic periods especially as the ageing or developing processes cause dental changes, and especially in middle age when the curvature of all our chin and lower jaw bones become more pronounced.

Emulation of another whose playing one admires will not necessarily be achieved by adopting identical equipment to them – although every salesman in the world will try to persuade you that this can be so! – and such changes of mouthpiece or instrument can actually be detrimental to the tone and to one's playing. Improvement will best be found to follow intelligent practise, and by working at technical problems calmly and honestly. It has been strongly advocated over the centuries that 'buzzing' gently and tunefully on the mouthpiece alone strengthens the embouchure and performs the daily 'warm-up' more effectively than anything else. It might be added that again it is beneficial to adopt the habit of applying as little pressure as possible whilst doing this, also to ensure that the tone is pure and trumpet-like. If this is done the instrument merely amplifies the result to good effect. If at any stage the trumpeter finds the tone coarse and 'growling', the impurity may be caused by the lip vibrating in two different places at two different speeds. This gives a double vibration in the mouthpiece (and instrument) producing an unpleasant sound which can be rectified virtually in seconds by 'buzzing' into the mouthpiece, listening hard, and eliminating the second unwanted vibration. ('Buzzing' without the mouthpiece is not recommended since it does not concentrate the lip vibrations where required; in this circumstance, once the mouthpiece is re-intoduced, surplus air tends to escape around the sides). This simple exercise may save some players hours of tedious 'limbering-up' especially when touring with an orchestra or band when practising time is limited.

Presuming that one is familiar and comfortable with one's trumpet, a few simple tests will quickly show whether the mouthpiece suits it. Firstly to gauge the response of it's lower register, and then for the higher notes one tests its production of the basic harmonics. It would be as well to test the harmonic notes against a keyboard instrument. It is important in particular to ensure that the octave C's are well centred, that the E's are not flat and that G in the stave is focused and that the G above it is not sharp. If any of these harmonics feel out of place they are likely to remain so and give continued problems once the valves are used. This is also a good test of a trumpet when using a familiar mouthpiece – they must match.

Twelve
Posture and Breathing

It is of extreme importance that the body is secure yet relaxed when standing or sitting to play.

When standing, the hips, knees and ankles should be allowed the necessary freedom to achieve an equal distribution of weight on the balls and the heels of the two feet; each foot should be positioned securely under its hip joint.

When sitting the legs should be folded in such a way as to rest the feet evenly on the floor with the toes and knees aligned in the same direction. The weight of the upper body should be evenly distributed onto the sitting bones. Do not lean on the back of the chair. The torso will receive all the support it needs from the spine and postural muscles when it is aligned with each vertebrae evenly separated from the one below it. This results in an upright posture which is free from unnecessary tension. The abdomen and arms are thus liberated for precise flexible movement required for the best possible co-ordination, and the breathing mechanism is left unaffected by misdirected postural tension.

The modern trumpet is generally constructed to be held in the left hand whilst the fingers of the right hand operate the valves. In addition to grasping the valve casing, the left hand usually has to operate a tuning slide for the third valve and sometimes one for the first valve also. This should be achieved as far as possible without transferring weight or grippage to the right hand whose little finger (called 'pinkie' in the USA) rests in a retaining ring. The trumpet may be held in the right hand whilst changes of mute are effected, but ideally the fingers retain more flexibility if relaxed and the right hand should merely rest along the instrument's mouthpipe. Some brass band and jazz musicians assert that if finger tips are used to depress the pistons, the involvement of additional finger joints slows the action which is speedier if a joint nearer the knuckles is used. This may indeed be so, but in the course of time the piston rod may become warped causing it to rub and stick against the apperture through which it passes into the valve casing.

When holding the instrument it is important that the upper body has an expanding potential whilst in the playing position. The shoulders need to release away from each other, and the elbows to release from the shoulders and each other in order that the muscles of the back will engage in the operation of supporting the arms and therefore the trumpet. This will make it possible to use the arms and respiratory system with the maximum efficiency yet the minimum of effort.

The cultivation of good breath control also assists in the process of muscular relaxation and helps to keep the brain clear and refreshed. The habit of inhaling frequent gulps of breath results in an accumulation of air in the lungs which does not have the opportunity of being expelled. This gives the performer the sensation of being 'out-of-breath' when in fact they have too much breath, but most of it de-oxygenated. When performing in public, nervousness induces tension in the lower abdomen and diaphragm; consequently the control of one's breathing falters, often with noticeable or embarrassing consequences. For this reason one should always be conscious of composing oneself both mentally and physically by fully exhaling and calmly replenishing the air in the lungs, perhaps being especially aware of the process in moments of apprehension. It is perhaps better to think that one is breathing into the instrument which is a natural act, as opposed to blowing into it which implies force.

As with many musical instruments, despite the best efforts of designers and manufacturers, the weight of a trumpet, and the angle at which it is held give rise to problems caused by muscular tension, especially after long, unbroken periods of playing or practicing. The angle at which the head is held, very often almost stooping forwards, strains the muscles of the upper neck, especially at the back of the head and at the base of the skull between the ears. To relieve this tension and prevent the muscles 'freezing', it is recommended that occasional recourse is taken to remedial exercises which will restore suppleness to the tissues.

Firstly, the head should be drawn backwards as if a book had been balanced on the top of the head – or even actually with a book so balanced. This entails also tucking in the chin, but the effect of such a manoeuvre is to stretch the muscles which hold the head [which is very heavy!] upright. A second useful method of relaxing this overworked area , is to draw in the chin in the same way, then turn the head slowly to the left as far as it will comfortably go, holding this posture for 3 or 4 seconds after which the forward facing position is regained. Next, perform exactly the same movement, but this time turning to the right, again holding for 3 or 4 seconds before returning to face forwards. This may be repeated 4 or 5 times. As a third exercise, place the right hand over the head to rest upon the left temple, [just in front of the left ear] whilst the head is again positioned with the chin drawn backwards [as if a book were on the head] then draw the head sideways towards the right shoulder; this stretches and frees up the muscles on the rear left side of the neck. Repeat this process with the left hand reaching to the right temple, and drawing the head towards the left shoulder. These motions may also be repeated 4 or 5 times.

A similar action draws the head forwards, alternating between the left and right elbows by turns being placed over the forehead whilst the left or right hand reaches backwards to the rear of the skull, whereupon the latter is gently pulled forwards towards the upper chest. All of these exercises will prevent the muscles which hold the head up from becoming too stiff.

The other part of the upper body which experiences tension from playing the trumpet, is across the shoulders and behind the shoulder blades. Many musicians, especially violinists, require courses of massage here, but one can stave off problems with movements which prevent the tissues from seizing up. Swimming is probably the most effective relaxation for muscles and joints in this part of the body, but simple arm stretches may help to offset trouble. Three of these are particularly helpful. Firstly, standing with feet slightly apart, both arms are raised directly upwards towards the ceiling, and the full stretch held for 15 to 20 seconds – stretching as far as possible, but without causing any sort of pain. This may be continued by stretching one arm at a time towards the ceiling, again as far as possible without pain.

Finally, it might be helpful to relax the shoulders by pulling both shoulder blades backwards and downwards, thereby exercising the muscles at the forward side of the shoulders; in this way all the tension caused by holding both arms in an unnaturally stiff, forward position whilst playing the trumpet, will be dispersed, and any stiffness eased.

Discomfort is also caused by inadequate or inappropriate nutrition. An excessively heavy meal with too much alcohol is not advisable before playing a musical instrument, neither is it sensible to starve the body of sustenance or fluid. Like athletes, musicians benefit from consuming energy-giving meals such as pasta; but eating food like beefsteak (which takes long to digest) and imbibing carbonated drinks may burn up the energy needed in the course of performance.

The following pages are devised to demonstrate how the author recommends that various instruments of the trumpet family should be held. This is not intended to be dogmatic but to be a helpful guide to aspiring performers, sometimes of rather obscure precursors of the modern instrument. It also gives more detailed pictures of these trumpets and guidance to anyone beginning to play them. Attention is especially given to the standing and sitting postures appropriate to each of them.

The regular modern trumpet should be held in the player's left hand. The thumb and middle finger may be required to operate tuning slides on the tubing of the first and third valves respectively.

The right hand is then placed with the fingertips of the three middle fingers over the tops of the three valves. The little finger [US pinkie] may rest lightly in a ring provided for that purpose, and the thumb rests against the casing of the first valve and under the lead-pipe.

The head should not be thrust forward into a 'stooping' posture; the elbows should not feel tense, also the back remains straight but relaxed, supported upwards from the hip joints. The shoulders should not be rounded and one should ensure that the shoulder blades are relaxed.

The weight should be evenly distributed between the heels and balls of the feet , both of which should be comfortably but securely positioned under its hip joint. One should feel no tension in the joints of the hips, knees or ankles.The stomach should not stick out.

The feet must be comfortable, either parallel or at a slightly divergent angle. If standing for long periods in hot temperatures it is advisable, when not playing, to gently [but imperceptibly] rock forwards and backwards to stimulate better circulation of the blood. Failure to do this occasionally causes players [especially bandsmen in cumbersome uniforms] to faint - this can be spectacularly embarrassing!

When seated a trumpeter should not lean against the back of the chair whilst playing; this hinders good breathing. The back should be kept straight and the shoulders composed into as relaxed a posture as possible; this allows the necessary expansion of the chest and lungs.

When seated the toes and knees of each leg should be aligned and the feet should rest evenly upon the floor. Again the stomach should not be pushed forwards.

The angle at which the trumpet is held may be determined by the player's dental formation. Not all trumpeters are comfortable holding the instrument level or parallel to the floor. A player with protuberant upper teeth may need to direct the trumpet downwards; others are happier playing 'upstream' .The important thing is to ensure maximum comfort and relaxation. At times players must be prepared to hold the bell of the trumpet up as a special visual effect; this also increases the apparent loudness since the sound is no longer absorbed by music desks or other musicians.

Those who wear spectacles should ensure that they can see both the music and the conductor clearly. Glasses which are too small, too heavy or unsuitably shaped may lead to postural problems.

In former times before valves, keys or slides were added, the trumpet was held firmly in one hand - usually but by no means always in the right hand. As on the pictured instrument, ornaments added to its decorative appearance, but audiences were most impressed by the fact that expressive, delicate musicianship could be achieved upon an item of military hardware !

Whist playing a 'Fanfare' or 'Baroque' trumpet a relaxed posture gives the player full control of his or her breathing system. The chest is not confined as it is when both hands are used, and the trumpet is held parallel to the ground [especially when a banner is suspended from it] facing either directly forwards or slightly to the right.. This gives even greater potential chest and lung expansion.

When a retractable rear slide was added to the trumpet in England at the end of the 18th century, the instrument was held by the left hand .The thumb rested on the 'crook', the three middle fingers were placed around the lead-pipe and the little finger [pinkie] gave additional balance.

Whilst playing the English slide-trumpet the performer's right hand needed to remain fairly relaxed to operate the mechanism effectively, but some of the weight was taken by the little finger [only] of the right hand which was positioned under the decorative pommel or 'ball'.

Previous observations regarding foot, ankle, knee, hip, back, shoulder and arm positions are just as relevant to old style instruments as modern ones.

Players who directed their instruments downwards were provided with a curved shank which was placed between the mouthpiece and crook; this permitted them to hold the trumpet level without discomfort or injury.

In England the earliest valves [two of them] were placed precisely where the slide pulley had previously been. The trumpet was therefore grasped in exactly the same way.

The right hand little finger likewise gave
additional support in holding the instrument.

By the second half of the 18th century some trumpets
were constructed in a double coil; although it looked
shorter this instrument had the same length of tubing
but was built in a more compact, possibly more convenient
shape. It was still grasped by the right hand. The trumpet
shown was made in St James' Street, London by Kohler
in the 1780s. Its mouthpiece and three crooks appear
contemporary with it. Eb trumpets in this shape are still used
in some regiments of the British army.

It was possible to reach with the left hand into the bell of the twice coiled trumpet. As upon the hand-horn it became a skilful art to manipulate the pitch of each note; they could all be lowered by a semitone and also the problematic 11th and 13th harmonics could be 'corrected'. [These were exactly the same notes which the slide trumpet could play but without the loss of tonal quality experienced with hand-stopping.]

Less alteration in tone is discernable if the left hand remains close to the bell on 'unstopped' notes. In theatres [this particular trumpet is believed to have associations with the Drury Lane theatre, London] its less penetrating tone may have been welcome - also its modest size.

In Vienna in the 1790s Anton Weidinger added keys to
a twice coiled trumpet. Most were subsequently made to be
played with the left hand and were therefore held with the
right, but some like the author's were constructed to be held
in the left hand leaving the right to operate the keys. The
prototype no longer survives, but it is assumed that it
possessed only three keys since the low note D [in concert
pitch] is noticeably missing from Haydn's 1796 concerto
[composed especially for Weidinger and his new 'invention'].
This note would have required a fourth key.

Weidinger's second design of keyed trumpet probably
had at least five keys [which are necessary for a
satisfactory performance of Hummel's concerto of 1803]
giving it a fully chromatic range together with some
desirable alternative fingerings. These keys occupy
all four fingers and the thumb of one hand; the
instrument must therefore be securely held by the other.

113

The 'Baroque Style' trumpet used nowadays looks strikingly like its ancestor. On the continent of Europe an instrument with three 'venting' holes is more common but in Britain a system employing four holes is found. Neither system was known in Baroque times and both are held with the left hand leaving the right to cover the finger-holes.

The finger-holes adjust certain harmonics; they also make the instrument safer to blow loudly, this consequently leads to misrepresentation of the trumpet's former 'noble' sound. These trumpets take either conventional modern mouthpieces or old-looking ones of 'modern' comfortable dimensions. They are likely therefore to merely amplify a 'modern' sound unless played with discernment.

In 1810 an Irish bandmaster, Joseph Halliday, patented
a fully chromatic keyed version of the military bugle, which
was then constructed in a single coil. The pictured 1823 bugle
has seven keys, five of which are operated with the right
hand and two by the left. For 40 years this instrument
achieved considerable musical success but was supplanted
upon the advent of the valved cornet.

When played in the standing position, the keyed bugle must be
supported by the end fingers of the left hand; the right hand
requires considerable dexterity throughout its range.

The Renaissance Cornetto employs seven finger-holes;
four are covered by the thumb and three fingers of the
left hand, three by three fingers of the right. It must be
stressed that the author's technique is unorthodox due
to the previously mentioned problem of a rather small
hand-stretch. The lowest hole for each hand has been
moved sideways to make them easier to reach.

Equally unorthodox is a large, trumpet-like mouthpiece.
In Renaissance times a much smaller one was often
used [the size of an acorn] which had a sharper rim. It
was usually played out of the corner of the mouth as
pictured in the chapter devoted to the Cornetto. In the
Hague, Holland, various original cornetto mouthpieces
may be examined; their sizes vary greatly, including a
few presumably used by musicians who also played the
trumpet, since they are surprisingly large.

The cornetto is also comfortable to play when seated. As with other instruments of the trumpet family, it is important to sit well and breathe freely – after all the cornetto was said to sound more like the human voice than any other musical instrument.

The [piston] Cornet has stood the test of time magnificently. Its shape has hardly altered in 150 years - a testament to the expertise of its early designers. Like most trumpets it is held in the left hand and played with the right.

Often regarded as ideal for beginners, the cornet is compact, sturdy and sweet-toned. The valves are positioned much nearer the player, therefore it is less difficult to hold for young musicians; it is also less cumbersome to carry.

As a popular and versatile solo instrument the cornet gives no undue problems when played standing. However the same principles of retaining good posture remain, especially since composers tend to give cornet players fewer bars rest than they give to trumpeters.

Posture and Breathing

Due to it's compact design
the cornet can comfortably be
held level by most players;
dental idiosyncrasies give less
marked differences in posture
than on longer instruments
of the trumpet family.
However the position of
the feet, ankles, knees and
back are equally important.
It is never good practice
to lean against the back of
a chair whilst playing.

Many early cornets had
no ring for the little finger
of the right hand;
this forestalls excessive
pressure being used in
the mistaken belief
that brute force will help
reaching higher notes.

The piccolo trumpet pitched in high Bb has a distinctive and vibrant tone. It is sometimes still used to perform Baroque music but has utterly different characteristics from the richly sonorous trumpets of Handel's time. In the dry, lifeless acoustics of many modern concert halls and studios its tone penetrates and dominates in the same way that a piccolo flute or high Eb clarinet does. Like most modern trumpets it is held with the left hand and the valves are operated by the right. Note that an additional 4th valve is fitted to extend its limited range downwards by a fourth.

Being small and compact the piccolo trumpet is comfortable to hold in both the standing and sitting positions, provided that good deportment is maintained. Increasing [sometimes excessive] use is made of this instrument in brass ensembles, therefore one should be prepared to exert the breathing system rather than risk loosening one's front teeth in one's efforts to satisfy those arrangers who are obsessed with interminable passagework of high notes. Good posture is essential.

The Rotary- valved trumpet is traditional to parts of Austria
and Germany. Its tone often suits Teutonic music well.
This type of valve disturbs the vibrating air column less than
a piston, but to the uninitiated such instruments are at
first less comfortable to hold. Usually the maker provides a
conveniently placed cross-bar so that the trumpet can be
securely held by the left hand.

On a Rotary-valved trumpet the right hand
operates the valves: sometimes a ring is provided
in which to rest the little finger.

Since the body of the Rotary- valved trumpet is broader, the chest of the player is less constrained by the action of drawing the hands inwards. For playing music of the 20th century, especially that written for film scores and the musical theatre, players must be ready to adjust their grip on the trumpet [even the hand in which they habitually hold it] to accommodate the rapid insertion of mutes.

Thirteen
Some Fundamental Points

Of all the wind and brass instruments, two may expect to reward the beginner with almost immediate, gratifying results. A student with a 'musical ear' can play a simple melody upon a recorder within minutes; likewise, it is far from rare for a first-time trumpeter or cornetist to produce a recognisable tune on their first day of playing. Technical fluency can be achieved on both of these far more quickly than upon a violin or flute, and yet only a few performers become publicly recognised as outstanding artists upon the simpler instruments in comparison with the many acclaimed virtuosi upon the latter. It is significant that at the end of the 18th century wind and brass instruments were developed that gave a greater range of notes, of dynamics, and most importantly of expression.

The recorder was left behind by modifications such as keys; the trumpet, though rendered fully chromatic by three valves, seemed banished to the back of the symphony orchestra where it now screams and snarls as a symbol of aggression. However in the inventive hands of jazz musicians and more recently in chamber ensembles and quintets, it has joined the cornet as a lyrical and expressive solo instrument in its own right. To provide a whole evening's entertainment upon the trumpet, players need to develop a palette of sound that is not wearying upon the ear of the listener, and an embouchure whose delicate muscles will not readily tire.

To this end the author is anxious to encourage aspiring recitalists to master the techniques of various members of the trumpet family, and to alternate between them both in practise and performance so that their audience may enjoy a varied repertoire from different historical periods, and may also appreciate the spectacle as much as the different sounds experienced.

The principle of note production of all trumpets, horns and tubas remains the same. The lips are placed upon the rim of a mouthpiece inside whose bowl (or 'cup') the apperture between the lips is caused to vibrate or 'buzz'. It is always good to practise this process into the mouthpiece alone, perhaps 'buzzing' a simple melody, and without applying undue pressure between the mouthpiece rim and the lip. The tone should be as trumpet-like as possible, and no superfluous hissing or non-vibrating air should be permitted to escape either at the sides of the mouth or from the stem of the mouthpiece where the vibrating air subsequently will enter the mouthpipe of the instrument. When a satisfactorily clear tone is achieved, the mouthpiece is placed into the instrument and simple modulations (or 'bugle calls') between the harmonics may be practised. The essence of all trumpet flourishes are to be found in such fanfares, and there is no finer exercise for this type of articulation. These should be played very quietly and cleanly as well as militarily to develop good tone and control.

Most players find that they require pressure to compress the lips sufficiently to produce the higher harmonics (often those above E in the stave).

This is only true to a very limited extent. In fact if too much pressure is applied, blood is squeezed from the lip and it ceases to vibrate at all. Moreover, the oxygen carried in the blood cells no longer reaches the delicate muscles through the veins and the muscular strength or support completely gives out. It is desirable therefore to play at all times with the minimum of mouthpiece pressure.

Many admirable techniques for developing the 'no-pressure' system have been devised. Amongst them suspending a cornet from the ceiling of a practise studio and balancing an instrument upon a pile of books on top of an upright piano. The method that seems most serviceable entails resting the trumpet upon each of one's thumbs in such a way that no grip or purchase can be made upon the body or cross-stays of the instrument. Usually the bell rests upon the upturned thumb of the left hand (ensuring that the index finger does not bend round to hold it) and the mouthpiece receiver balances upon the right thumb, again ensuring that it is not held either before or during the exercise.

The trumpet or cornet may now be held at precisely the same angle to the face and embouchure that is customary to the player. A low 'C' should be played with a full tone, but not too loudly. This should be held as a 'long note' without allowing superfluous air to escape around the mouthpiece rim and the sound should resonate with absolute purity. Subsequently, the same low 'C' is produced in the same way, but once resonating well the lips are tightened and the flow of air slightly increased to raise the note to the next upward harmonic (the note, middle 'G') and held – again as a 'long note' and with as clear and pure a tone as possible. The following stage is to recommence with low 'C', again not too loudly but with free (unbreathy) sound, to raise the note through 'G' in the stave to 'C' in the third space from the bottom of the stave.

Thereafter, returning each time to a clearly produced low 'C' the player raises the note by one harmonic each time and holding the final note for as long as is comfortable and without inducing pressure.

It may be that at the first attempt, only two or three harmonics work with this method, but if one perseveres it is possible to proceed to the next adjacent harmonic in a few days time – it does not matter how long it takes or how high it goes, the importance of the exercise is to develop strength and confidence over a period of time, and to develop the muscular tissue so that there is no 'break' in the embouchure between the low and upper registers. In time it is possible to cover two and a half or even three octaves with this method, leaving the player with endurance and even tone throughout the trumpet's range.

A word of warning is necessary however. It is imperative that the above exercise is not started in the middle or upper register – ALWAYS bottom 'C' must be the starting note, otherwise there is a strong tendency for the player to develop a 'phoney' embouchure which usually manifests itself in tucking the lower lip underneath the upper which leads to a 'break' between upper and lower registers, and invariably to an eventual total collapse in the upper part of the range.

This system has sometimes been criticised for not developing the very loud playing often required of the modern trumpeter, but what can be achieved quietly can simply be amplified by an increased supply of air. What many players fail to realise is that the reverse of this process is not true – those who only play and practice very loudly lose all control and flexibility at reduced volume and the complete player must be able to do both. Increased air pressure needs to be supported by the lower abdomen if it is not to be harmful (or to invite muscular rupture as in the conspicuous case of the late Dizzie Gillespie). An extremely beneficial and simple exercise in developing the necessary diaphraghmatic control is to play simple scales slowly over two octaves (up and down) without starting the note with the tongue, but by 'huffing' each note with air support only. Again, this does not need to be loud necessarily, but when first put into practice the player may feel light-headed from employing and developing regions of the lung's capacity which have never previously been exercised, and it is advisable to start either seated, or in a position where the player is unlikely to be injured should a fit of fainting occur.

Some teachers attempt to standardise the ideal placement of the mouthpiece rim upon the lips. The problem with such an approach is that each individual has different dental structure and distribution of both facial muscles and thickness of exposed lip tissue. Therefore generalisations are often unhelpful and the essential requirement is that the lips are permitted to vibrate comfortably and completely; in other words, in such a way that all the air in the body of the trumpet or cornet is set into vibrating motion – this is what creates a clear pure sound. When some of the air column is not vibrating freely, the sound becomes dull or 'fuzzy' and it is more important that this impurity of tone is eliminated than that the mouthpiece sits precisely centrally on the face and equally distributed between the upper and lower lip. Ideally, of course, if the mouthpiece is central, the distribution of muscular control is balanced between right and left sides of the face; but like left and right hands and feet, arms and legs, eyes and ears, nature does not always balance these equally and most people find one side of the face slightly stronger than the other. The most important muscles that require development to give a trumpet player control over all registers of the instrument are those around the chin and those of the cheeks under the eyes. It will be found that these are greatly developed by simple mouthpiece practice and the long-note exercise with the trumpet balanced on the thumbs previously described.

There are many books of study available for the development of lip flexibility and of extended routines for 'warming up'. If you find these helpful and beneficial then you should by all means take full advantage of them. I have to admit that I have never had recourse to such books, finding them lacking in musical interest and tending (like weight lifting) to make the muscles stiff and inflexible, encouraging brute force to replace suppleness.

It is the upper register of the trumpet in which many players have difficulty gaining and maintaining their confidence. To some extent this has been mentally preconditioned by the majority of study books such as the great J.B. Arban's 'Method' (the trumpet/cornet player's 'bible') which rarely ascends to the second octave 'C' ♯≣ and only occasionally reaches the notes B♮, B♭ and A below it – certainly never developing a sense of 'tessitura' in this register or exploring the octave above it. Some of Arban's immediate successors were able to cover a range of four chromatic octaves on the cornet and recent re-mastered recordings of 'live' concert performances bear astonishing testament to their abilities.

All too often aspiring players avoid practising the extremeties of the trumpet's range, but the fact is that without practise neither very high nor very low notes will appear from nowhere. Below low F♯ the modern player is not often required to play (F♮ is needed in Bizet's *Carmen*, Chabrier's *España* and Schumann's 3rd Symphony) and certainly no great kudos may be anticipated from being able to play this register well, but the florid register above high B♮ is fully utilised in music of the Baroque period which is a constant source of delight to audiences and a lucrative source of income to a dependable performer. However, at some period the player will undoubtedly be expected to play low notes and if they have disappeared off one's range they can easily be restored by the simple expedient of articulating gently into the mouthpiece the following sequences of notes, subsequently playing them upon the trumpet (or cornet).

(To play F♮ clearly, one should fully extend the 1st and 3rd valve slides).

An equally straightforward exercise may be used for consolidating the high register, but it should be emphasised that at no time should the player continue if the notes do not speak cleanly. As with the 'huffing' development of lower abdominal muscles, the player should initially work on this study in a sitting position, or where no damage or injury will occur in the event of over-exertion. A further important observation is that bars of respite have been written into these exercises, and they form an essential part of them since a period of resuscitation and replenishment of oxygen greatly helps develop endurance and stamina. The author firmly rejects former methods' where revival was discouraged – such a system ultimately leads to reliance upon brute force and may also permanently impair muscular tissue.

This exercise, if approached sensibly, will greatly help to extend the average player's range and confidence in the higher register; in theory, it could be extended indefinitely. It may

be timely also to suggest a constructive method of preparing Baroque repertoire, especially for performers who are required to play this music infrequently. Bach's second Brandenburg Concerto requires the solo trumpeter to play in the higher register not only with little rest but also with such delicacy that the sound of a recorder (playing much of the time a third below the trumpet) is not obscured. The work is not a Trumpet Concerto, but a Concerto Grosso in which four instruments, violin, oboe, recorder and trumpet are equal partners. I often hear trumpeters omitting the less melodic, low-lying passages of the work, but Bach clearly intended these notes as an integral part of the music, and in any case, it is psychologically undermining to admit to oneself that you cannot play the work properly. It is better, in my opinion, to prepare the piece in stages some weeks in advance, omitting nothing. However, it is not essential to play this concerto in the practise room without substantial rests which will permit the muscles to revive and to eventually develop the required endurance.

BMV 1047 Brandenburg Concerto No. 2.

To examine this piece in detail might be helpful. The first 12 bars should be reasonably straightforward, although the trill in bars 3 and 4 needs to be both neat and discreet. In bar 15 one encounters the highest notes and they need to be articulated cleanly; whether a soft stroke of the tongue is employed, or slurring, or pairing of notes, may ultimately depend upon the approach of the other three soloists; one should ideally be prepared to accomodate the other players. Due to the unusual demands made upon the trumpeter however, most other musicians (but not all!) will accept the phrasing adopted by the trumpet player. If one or two notes do not 'speak' to your satisfaction, play the passage again (after a brief pause) until they do work – then continue. With most students the following 6 bars flow quite naturally but bars 25 and 26 are problematic. In this event, take a rest and recommence in bar 24 with a fresh 'lip' and when you are ready play bars 25 and 26 cleanly.

Konzert D - Dur

fur D Trompete, Streicher und Cembalo

On the following day, begin this passage at bar 23, and the next day take it back to bar 21; subsequently (hopefully) you will soon be able to play the passage from bars 19 to 28 without a break. Working at this piece in small sections, gradually tying them together eventually enables the trumpeter to play the whole work without leaving chunks of it out. This approach may also usefully be applied to the opening movements of the trumpet concerti of Telemann and Molter, also to passages of Bach's *Mass in B Minor* and other standard movements of the trumpet's repertoire. It is a good discipline also to prepare one-self to play the second and third trumpet parts of Bach's orchestral and choral music, since they make slightly different demands, and have their own technical challenges. At some stage in most players' careers, they are required to play in a trumpet section, and this is a very rewarding and satisfying

CONCERTO No. 1

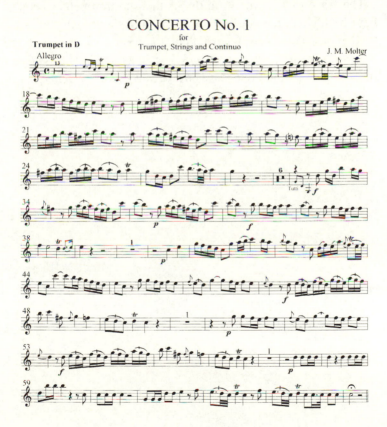

133

experience if done well. Moreover an accurate and supportive second trumpet is always in demand as a colleague.

Whilst the author's thoughts are dwelling upon points of professional etiquette, it cannot be too strongly emphasised that nothing is more irritating, off-putting or disrespectful to colleagues than a 'bandroom soloist'. Avoid the temptation to demonstrate your entire concerto repertoire in the dressing room prior to a performance; if you could play the pieces that well, you wouldn't be in the bandroom but in the soloist's suite. Other members of the ensemble are often trying to make last-minute adjustments to their instruments, and this is neither the time nor the place for the exercise of an 'ego'.

The reason why I mention this is that the trumpeter needs to have built his or her confidence inside, and should have no need to demonstrate it elsewhere than its proper place upon the platform. In the following pages I shall endeavour to suggest other ways in which one may ensure that this confidence is not misplaced.

Fourteen
Articulation

Whatever musical style or idiom is chosen by the aspiring trumpeter, it will be essential to blend with other performers who produce sound in a different way. Often the trumpet is expected to punctuate the texture with firm rhythmic precision, but a 'legato' style is required if imitating a singer; here the notes need to be stroked and articulated softly, or even slurred in an unbroken line as is often heard on a stringed instrument.

The first of these ways of producing sound is achieved by the tip of the tongue regulating the flow of air immediately behind the teeth. It used to be likened to spitting a raspberry pip from between the lips, but teachers are careful nowadays to ensure that this process does not actually impede air passing through the mouth into the trumpet as opposed to controlling the airstream; this is particularly significant in the context of the 21st century when volume levels have increased substantially since the introduction of electronic instruments and sound systems. It is generally still held that the syllable 'Tu, Tu, Tu' or 'Ta, Ta, Ta', at the beginning of the notes produces the desired effect, as admirably described in J.B. Arban's great 'Method'. Remember however to pronounce 'Tu' in the short French way as opposed to the long English 'Too, Too, Too'.

Arban and his contemporaries did not approve of the 'stroked' articulation which may be described as employing the syllable 'Du, Du, Du' or 'Da, Da, Da'; this was considered to be a very 'lazy' option, but in 'swing' it is an essential articulation to fit the style of the music.

Likewise, the unbroken 'legato' may sound very relaxed, but

is a very demanding technique if it breaches the harmonic sequences and if it is not to sound vulgar. The tone has to be continuous and even, as if the unbroken sound 'Aaaaaaaa . . .'

The same phrase articulated in these ways results as follows:

TaTaTaTaTaTaTaTa   TaTaTaTaTa   —DaDaDaDaDaDaDaDa   DaDaDaDaDa   —A - - - - - - - - - - -

Some sequences of notes lend themselves to all three modes of articulation:

Ta Ta Ta Ta Ta Ta Ta Ta   Ta Ta Ta Ta Ta ———
Da Da Da Da Da Da Da Da   Da Da Da Da Da ———
A - - - - - - - -   - - - - - - ———

Other phrases are characteristic of specific means of production:

Ta   TaTaTaTa   TaTa   Ta TaTaTa   TaTa   Ta TaTaTa   TaTa   Ta ——

Da   Da Da   Da   Da Da Da   Da   Da Da   Da   Da Da Da ——

Aa — Aa   Aa   A - a - a - a   Aa   Aa   A - a - a - a   Aa - Aa   A - a - a - a   Aa —

At any time the professional player must be ready to set the mood to 'martial', 'swing' or 'ballad' in this way. One must also be ready for an articulation which is particularly well suited to the trumpet – double and triple tonguing. These are often neglected by those with a naturally rapid single tongue, sometimes at their peril because sooner or later the technique will be required of them, and without regular practise or application it becomes uneven and 'bumpy'. It is advisable to practise both of these rather slowly from time to time in order to ensure that the adjacent syllables are even and rhythmical. All too often consecutive notes that should be of equal value sound uneven, or as if they are dotted. The syllables are formed in the throat as 'Tu-Ku, Tu-Ku, Tu-Ku, Tu-Ku, Ta—' or 'Ta-Ka, Ta-Ka, Ta-Ka, Ta-Ka, Ta—' if required to be crisp. Likewise in legato they sound: 'Du-Gu, Du-Gu, Du-Gu, Du-Gu, Da—' or 'Da-Ga, Da-Ga, Da-Ga, Da-Ga, Da—'.

Triple tonguing can be produced as any of the following syllables:

'Tu-Tu-Ka, Tu-Tu-Ka, Tu-Tu-Ka, Tu-Tu-Ka, Ta—'

'Ta-Ta-Ke, Ta-Ta-Ke, Ta-Ta-Ke, Ta-Ta-Ke, Ta—'

'Tu-Ka-Ta, Tu-Ka-Ta, Tu-Ka-Ta, Tu-Ka-Ta, Ta—'

'Ta-Ke-Ta, Ta-Ke-Ta, Ta-Ke-Ta, Ta-Ke-Ta, Ta—'

The student should find by trial and error which of these articulations best suit him or her and stick to it! Again, it is beneficial to start very slowly and gradually speed the exercise up. First one should repeat the same note, then adjacent notes, then runs and finally interval leaps:

Double and triple tonguing are extremely easy to speed up once the knack is acquired but exceedingly difficult to slow down, therefore I repeat that patient practise at slow speeds will yield gratifying results. Frequently during a performance, a conductor will become excited during a passage that he has carefully rehearsed at a comfortable speed for single-tonguing, but which then falls 'into the slot' between single- and double-; the player who can readily fall back upon controlled double-tonguing will not be found wanting. Moreover, in the accoustics of a very large building, double-tonguing does not tend to interrupt the flow of air between the teeth as much as single-tonguing and therefore sound projection is much easier.

Other effects may be worth mentioning in passing such as flutter-tonguing or 'growling' which is occasionally demanded. This is achieved by rolling the tongue as if pronouncing repeated R's (Rrrrrr . . .) whilst still blowing into the trumpet. It becomes impracticable in the extreme registers of the instrument. Notes can be 'bent' and 'glissando' or 'sliding' achieved whilst the valves are imperfectly depressed. Sometimes called a 'smear' this sound can be very effective when well executed, as demonstrated by the late Eddie Calvert in his famous rendition of the melody 'Cherry Pink and Apple Blossom White'.

Whilst on the subject of interesting gimmicks, it is possible, if so desired to develop indefinite endurance (provided the embouchure holds out) upon the trumpet by means of circular- or rotary-breathing. This entails drawing air in through the nose whilst continuing to exhale into the trumpet – an essential ingredient in the technique of playing the Australian didgeridoo. An introduction may be effected by taking a glass of water and a straw through which bubbles may be blown to the water's surface whilst air is drawn into the cheeks from the nostrils. The lungs will require a certain amount of air also, therefore one has to alternate between lung breathing and cheek blowing. The musical benefits of this technique are dubious because so many pieces entail imitation of vocal phrases which naturally shape themselves like a spoken sentence. Without the punctuation of breathing points the music tends to loose its sense of structure and devolves into a succession of phraseless sounds which have rhythm and pitch but no meaning.

Chapter 15
Detailed Preparations

Having just completed (as I write) the most demanding project of my professional career, exhorted by my colleagues, I am emboldened to recall in detail, the experience of preparation preceding it, hoping that it may serve as a helpful document of guidance to other trumpeters confronted by the challenge of 'uncharted waters'.

The enterprising record company Hyperion, noted for adventurous forays into unexplored musical territory, undertook in January 2001 to record the Trumpet concertos of Haydn and Hummel, featuring the instrument for which they were originally composed, the Keyed-Trumpet. The orchestral accompaniment was to be provided by one of the world's finest 'Period Music' ensembles, The King's Consort under the direction of their founder Robert King. Having worked with these fine players for many years, it was for me a happy choice, and my aspirations were, in the event, well founded. Other items on the programme were works from the same historical period, by Michael Haydn (Joseph's younger brother) JW Hertel and Leopold Mozart (Wolfgang's father, also, interestingly, a sometime trumpeter himself).These three pieces all ascend to the highest register of the Natural Trumpet in contrast especially to Hummel's masterpiece, which for the first time explored the melodic possibilities of the lowest register.

The two main concertos were not unfamiliar to me in their historical guise. Haydn's has received at least ten public performances from me, six of which were in the USA followed in England at festivals in Bridgenorth, Oxford, Warwick and

The Trumpet

Cheltenham. The work is in the key of E♭ and is playable on a trumpet with only 3 keys. Hummel's on the other hand requires at least 5 keys, possibly (as proved to be necessary) more, the tonality in this case being half a tone higher in E. Previous performances had been undertaken separately, allowing plenty of time to acclimatise to the instrument's idiosyncracies in each key. However, they now had to prepared "back-to-back" which proved problematic, since the fingerings were slightly, but confusingly, different .

Apart from the technical headaches posed, there was clearly going to be the need for unusual resources of stamina, since we had 6 hours on three consecutive days to complete our task. This tough schedule is not uncommon due to the financial strictures of renting an appropriate hall, and engaging the best musicians whilst they are available.

Robert King and I selected and ran through the repertoire some six months beforehand. This was necessary in order to establish the timings of each piece, and to assure ourselves of their suitability. It also enabled me to check the tuning of certain notes in great detail; this may seem obvious, but in performance, one has a degree of latitude upon an old-style instrument, when the audience can see that it is not a conventional one. On a CD one must remember that the results of one's efforts will be heard on the radio, in the car and upon airline headphones, therefore the result must bear scrutiny by the listening faculties alone, no excuses or explanations being acceptable for any deficiencies. An additional dimension presents itself in that during this particular epoch, the pitch of orchestral instruments in Austria (where they were first played) lay somewhere between modern pitch[A= 440] and Baroque pitch (A= 415) at A= 430. This is initially uncomfortable to musicians, let alone to listeners. Over the ensuing weeks, despite the customary rush of Xmas pageants and Carol concerts, the various pieces were kept 'on the boil' with regular practise to keep them fresh. Three weeks before recording began, intensive preparations started in earnest.

I first enlisted the help of my long-standing friend and colleague, the keyboard virtuoso Leslie Pearson, to whose house I took an appropriately re-tuned keyboard. For several hours we worked painstakingly through each movement of every piece, adjusting certain notes and seeking improved fingerings; also we checked the technical fluency of intricate passages. We were surprised that so few problems arose which were not solvable, and I returned home in buoyant spirits and in a confident frame of mind.

I was apprehensive that once human elements were added to the equation, the tuning of orchestral instruments would not relate as precisely to the synthesised sounds with which we had been working. Over the following days therefore, I worked alone in my own studio using a metronome and cassette recorder only, and recorded each movement, endeavouring to perfect every passage and phrase in anticipation of what would be required of me in a few day's time. This process was a great shock, and a very demoralising experience. The evident unevenness of the Keyed-Trumpet's tone between those notes played with keys closed and those with them open, and the lack of fluency of fast passages when played directly into a close microphone, both required remedial attention. Likewise, the florid high 'tessitura' in the lesser known works were not as accurate or secure as they had felt on each occasion of running through them with a keyboard.

The first matter to be dealt with was the lack of resonance once certain keys were opened. On woodwind instruments, the size of the holes perforating the body of it's tubing is a very important factor, both for intonation and tone. So too is the height to which it's covering keypad is raised. In the Hummel concerto , it became imperative to re-invent the fingering of several notes since sometimes two holes opened simultaneously greatly improved matters. One hole in particular needed to be reduced to half it's former diameter, and four of the six keys needed to have a contrivance fitted whereby their height could be adjusted for the different pitches of E and E♭. (The trumpet originally had 5 keys, but a 6th was added to obtain one particularly elusive note – this subsequently transpired to solve other difficulties). The new device consisted of an adjustable, lockable screw with a cork pad mounted upon it (to avoid clicking or tapping being picked up by the microphones). After this the new fingerings had to be practised to fluency, and mental preparedness for subsequent alterations set in readiness. Once recording actually commenced many further adjustments had to be made, so it was all to the good that a great deal of thought had already been applied into solving these details.

The technically difficult music was improved by the time-honoured process of firstly reducing the tempo substantially, and thereafter gradually increasing it until accuracy was achieved at the desired speed; secondly, passages may be dismembered into small constituent parts, which are perfected separately, then progressively joined together into longer sections until ultimately the entire section may be played with assurance.

The remaining matter requiring preparation was developing the necessary stamina. Since the Keyed-Trumpet has a rather diffuse, unfocussed tone, the player's lip has to create each note, compensating for varying degrees of tonal purity. This is much more strenuous to the small muscles of the face than normal trumpeting. Moreover, these delicate tissues bruise easily, and once swollen will not vibrate freely. A balance has therefore to be struck between being in perfect physical readiness for the days of continuous blowing, and over-exertion which might severely impair one's ability to play with any degree of control or refinement.

On this occasion it would not have been appropriate to take recourse to the brass player's usual solution to stamina problems, which is to transfer support from the facial muscles to those of the breathing system and the diaphragm. This is because the essential characteristic of trumpet music of this period is its surprising softness of tone, and the ability to blend with the softer instruments of the orchestra, such as flutes and clarinets. We must accept, however reluctantly, that the strident, aggressive sound associated nowadays with the trumpet, was unknown in the context of art music in the 18th century, and the breathing techniques developed in the early 20th century (initially by singers, coping with large, unreverberant opera houses) are not appropriate to music of this earlier period. Also, if trumpets with keys or vent-holes are blown too forcibly into a microphone, the disparity between vented and unvented (open and closed) holes becomes uncomfortably apparent to the dicerning listener. The 'art' is to disguise not to accentuate this limitation; previous attempts at recording this repertoire upon recreations of historic instruments have been judged not to have overcome this problem convincingly.

In many of my own previous recordings I have used larger mouthpieces from the 18th and 19th centuries, to cultivate that velvety, unbrazen quality which I believe to have characterised British trumpet-playing in earlier centuries. These are not designed for 'running around' the upper register as required in the music of Bach and Michael Haydn, for which a shallower mouthpiece is generally required. On this occasion, when my lips grew severely tired, I resorted to a German-made mouthpiece for a few of the very highest passages of Hertel and Michael Haydn's concertos.

The results of these strenuous endeavours have yet to be heard or judged, but certainly no greater exertion could have been made to ensure success, nor can a recording of trumpet music have been provided with the accompaniment of better, or more supportive orchestral playing.

The author also hopes that in reading of these experiences, others will have gained an insight into one player's methods of preparation, and be helped to approach their own projects without succumbing to panic or neurosis!

Sixteen
And finally…

There are certain aspects of one's musical development which cannot be left to chance, but which opportunity may help to develop more quickly. Most necessary of all is a good technique, which can only be acquired with concentrated practise, and good quality practise. This means working at things that one finds hard, not playing the familiar tunes to impress the neighbours. Long hours are not essential, but difficult areas of technique will not resolve themselves without application, and a golden rule is to never put the instrument away until you have played to your own complete satisfaction passages that trouble you. This means that if a high note won't speak, or an awkward run of notes defies you, do not say to yourself 'it'll be better tomorrow, maybe' because without being sorted out it won't. Even if you play a passage under speed, or approach a high note from only a bar before it (assuming it occurs at the end of a long phrase) do not allow yourself not to play it right.

It is often very boring to have to practise repetitive technical exercises; frequently there is not an ounce of music in them, this is technique for technique's sake. However, it is necessary to have good and complete facility upon your instrument, especially if you intend to work in music that requires improvisation – the greatest players in this field never seem to stop working away at obscure corners of their technique. It is good discipline for any player to spend 10 to 15 minutes (only) daily in brushing up awkward fingerwork.

It is also essential to read and transpose at sight. Many students apply themselves to books of orchestral excerpts, but nothing improves awareness better than experience because so often it is not what you have to play that matters but when you have to play it. The context of an exposed entry after many bars and minutes of inactivity makes orchestral trumpet playing surprisingly nerve-racking at times. Many, many excellent orchestral players have made their way into the profession through the brass band movement where they have developed extraordinary technical fluency, and nerves of steel from the experience of contests. It comes as a shock sometimes when they join an orchestra, where only one player covers each part, and though no demands are made of their technical skills, the playing of a solitary note will cause a flute player to give a sour look because he (or she) thinks that note is not blending with someone else's. Continuous exposure to this sort of ordeal has made life stressful for more than one outstanding trumpeter.

Those moving from the world of 'banding' to the sphere of orchestral playing often encounter criticism in the use of vibrato. I personally enjoy a degree of lyricism upon the trumpet, but find myself very uncomfortable with vibrato in music where it does not fit the style. The music of Gabrieli or his contemporaries of the late 16th century is killed stone dead in my opinion by the first hint of 'wobble'; likewise, the trumpet music of Restoration London loses all its serenity and dignity by self-indulgent excess of ornamentation. To play dance and theatre music of the 1930's and 1940's 'straight' and without feeling for the style, leaves it stillborn and it is therefore instructive to listen to, play with and to learn from as many top-class players as you can, appreciating their diversity of styles.

There are some obvious 'do's' and 'don'ts' whilst on or near the concert platform which, despite the risk of repeating myself, are worth mentioning. Firstly, ensure that your instrument is in good working order. This includes verifying that the valves and slides are clean and well oiled or greased. The internal tubing and inside the mouthpiece's throat and stem should be regularly cleared of residual matter! Lack of attention to this detail can ultimately cause total blockage, and in any case the bacteria which gather and breed can be exceedingly unhealthy; throat infections and lip sores are an almost inevitable consequence of neglect of hygiene.

The water-key area needs special attention since the water escape hole can easily become blocked; it is worth checking also that the cork, springs and mechanisms which operate it are in good condition and clean. For those intrepid players who venture to perform upon instruments of the 19th century with keys, ensure that the leather pads are not too dry; the leather responds well to moistening and this is especially necessary if the instrument has not been played for some time.

Shining silver plate or bright lacquer certainly gives a good initial impression to an onlooker and this may be very important. Experienced players however are reluctant to have an 'old friend' tampered with since we all know tales of trumpets which never played as well again having been rebuilt or reconditioned. On un-lacquered or un-plated instruments polishing fractionally reduces the thickness of the metal every time cleaning is undertaken and it is therefore undesirable if not irresponsible to continually bring a brass instrument of any antiquity to a shiny state; it is also foolish to permit such an instrument to tarnish to the point of corrosion.

Springs do not often need replacing, but when they do it is essential to find the right size and shape since valves and slides do not function efficiently with springs of incorrect dimension and tension. If mutes are used frequently their corks require periodic replacement – again it is important that these replacements are of exactly the correct size otherwise the intonation and response of the mute may not be satisfactory.

Once you are confident that the instrument is in perfect working order it is also important that you present yourself well to the audience. Walk on stage calmly – this will give the onlooker the impression that you have confidence in yourself. You may not necessarily feel this yourself but it will help to engender a feeling of calm and self-assurance. To know that you are smartly dressed will additionally induce a sense of well-being, especially if you are conspicuously visible at the front of the stage.

It is not many years since it was perceived as being fashionable or 'cool' to look rather scruffy on stage; I maintained then, and still do, that this may be interpreted as showing a lack of respect to the ticket-buying public. I suggest further that it may reveal a lack of self-worth in the performing artist. Some of the very greatest musicians have the misfortune to resemble a sackful of potatoes whatever efforts are made to smarten them up, but deliberate or careless slovenliness is another matter. My intimate colleagues will laugh aloud upon reading these words, recalling my own sartorial inadequacies in the past, but I write with the crusading zeal of a reformed character.

Once on stage and preparing to play, direct the sound towards the audience and not into the folds of a music stand. Hold the instrument up as high as is comfortable and ensure that the preparatory intake of breath is both measured and full; take care also that the instrument is raised to the lips in good time before playing, not jerked into position at the very last moment.

From time to time water which has condensed in the tubing needs to be expelled. This operation should be carried out as discreetly and indiscernibly as possible; resist the urge to puff and hiss loudly whilst blowing this water out in the course of a quiet restful passage of music which does not involve you. Early trumpets and cornets gathered this moisture in the crooks placed between the mouthpiece and the lead-pipe, the crook could therefore be surreptitiously removed and emptied almost imperceptibly. A water-key is placed at the lowest and most forward part of the instrument's front bow where moisture gathers in a modern instrument. It is also almost as distant from the player and as near as the audience as the bell and is therefore more noticeable when emptied unless one is circumspect in the process. This is most frequently a problem with the vented Baroque-style trumpet upon which water is removed via the rearmost [thumb] hole. If blown out forcefully, as is generally the case, the audience can become severely distracted from the more important musical activities taking place. I have found that holding the instrument for a few seconds at the appropriate angle will permit the water to flow away of its own accord without making a great palaver of it!

It is only natural to feel nervous before performing in public; indeed it is unnatural not to do so and nervous adrenaline sharpens and focuses the concentration in a most productive way. However until one is familiar and confident with an audience, it is advisable to be conscious of avoiding those mannerisms which reveal the anxiety which would be better kept to yourself. When standing, avoid fidgeting or transferring the weight from one leg to the other too frequently. It also does not look good if you allow a foot to tap; both these habits can be cured by concentrating upon resting the weight evenly upon the flat part of both feet.

A further manifestation of insecurity reveals itself when players are 'edgy' with their colleagues or others working with them such as recording or lighting engineers. This includes aggressiveness and apparent arrogance, or the constant seeking to be the centre of attention. Other musicians do not wish to have their time or energy wasted, or to feel that their own contributions are less valid or worthy. A confident, secure person gives reassurance to those around him [her], conversely someone who is insecure invariably [even if unwittingly] tends to unsettle others. It is a simple factor of life that if people enjoy the experience of working with you then they are far more likely to wish to repeat that experience than if they have not enjoyed it.

Courtesy and politeness should also be extended to those seeking to employ you. A swift response to a letter or message is always appreciated and most employers like a decisive reply, which if affirmative is held as a commitment. Any working musician knows that this is not always possible and moreover that this commitment is too often regarded by unscrupulous employers as one sided. However it is usually best to be honest and straightforward if there are possible problems of conflicting obligations.

And finally...

Keep your working diary updated all the time, otherwise you may miss out in a competitive market-place where others (who you may even consider to be less talented than yourself) are better organised. The same goes for keeping your business accounts; I and innumerable colleagues have formerly fallen into the trap of letting such matters slide, with the uncomfortable result that eventually the accounts have to be settled and agreed with the revenue authorities, and tedious as it is, the only mature way to cope with this is to be as disciplined about this as you should be with your daily practise. The saying amongst London musicians has always been: 'Art for Art's sake, but money for God's sake'. I hope that my readers will derive great pleasure from the former, and if they achieve the latter in the process, so much the better.

Trinity & All Saints

ACCREDITED BY THE UNIVERSITY OF LEEDS

LIS LIBRARY

This book is due for return on or before the last date
stamped below

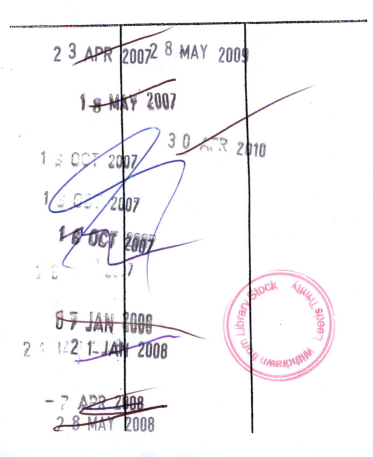